Endorsements

We live in a day where the word is being preached like never before. Through radio, television, Internet, podcasts, and a myriad of other avenues people have the opportunity to receive the life-giving message of the Gospel. Why is it that the church seems more anemic and powerless than ever before? The problem is not the seed, it is the soil! Join Daniel Norris as he articulately describes how to properly receive and respond to the Word of God. These life-changing principles will propel you into a new arena of relationship with the Lord Jesus and start a fresh revival in your heart!

JOEL STOCKSTILL
Bethany Church, Baton Rouge, LA

Jesus declared that "man does not live on bread alone but on every word that comes from the mouth of God." The quality of our life is not based upon our occupation or monetary status but upon our ability to hear the voice of God. Daniel Norris does an excellent job of helping develop one's ability to identify and hear God's voice. Your relationship with the Lord will be strengthened and spiritual life enhanced as you enjoy this inspirational book.

PASTOR RICHARD CRISCO
Rochester First, Rochester, MI

Following in the footsteps of his mentor Steve Hill, Daniel Norris has written a no-compromise, no-nonsense manual that will help you remove the obstacles that stand between you and an effective life of service in the kingdom of God. Read this book and you will be challenged, inspired, and encouraged.

DR. MICHAEL BROWN
President, FIRE School of Ministry

receptivity

receptivity

TUNING IN TO GOD'S VOICE

daniel k. norris

DESTINY IMAGE® PUBLISHERS, INC.
P.O. Box 310, Shippensburg, PA 17257-0310
"Promoting Inspired Lives."

This book and all other Destiny Image and Destiny Image Fiction books are available at Christian bookstores and distributors worldwide.

Cover design by Eileen Rockwell

For more information on foreign distributors, call 717-532-3040.
Reach us on the Internet: www.destinyimage.com.

ISBN 13 TP: 978-0-7684-0704-4
ISBN 13 eBook: 978-0-7684-0705-1

For Worldwide Distribution, Printed in the U.S.A.
1 2 3 4 5 6 7 8 / 19 18 17 16 15

Dedication

Dedicated in loving memory to my friend and mentor Evangelist Steve Hill—the burning ember that sparked that great move of God in Pensacola, Florida. You touched the world. May we strive to follow in your footsteps.

No eye has seen, no ear has heard, no mind has conceived
what God has prepared for those who love him.
—Isaiah 64:4

Contents

Foreword

by Steve Hill

Daniel Norris is a *John the Baptist* screaming in the wilderness to the young and old alike. The church desperately needs such voices in these last days. In a few short years the generals of the past will begin to fade. A younger generation will seek out these risky radicals who are fired-up fanatics, not phony fakes. Daniel is blazing a trail for millions of these spiritual wanderers.

From the onset of my Christian walk, I have had the privilege of being trained and mentored by some of the most stalwart men of God of our generation. I'm eternally grateful for David Wilkerson, Leonard Ravenhill, and other spiritual generals who personally poured into my life and helped shape me into a man of God. These men were keenly aware of their God-given responsibility to raise up others who would carry on the work of the Lord.

Over the years, I have endeavored to follow their example by pouring myself into men and women who have the call of God upon their lives. That's why I mentor men like Daniel. That's why Ravenhill mentored me. I was rough, I was radical, and I was *ready*. He was right in picking me as a Timothy.

He plowed, he planted, and he prayed. The harvest has been incredible.

Daniel and his wife Jenna first sat under our ministry at the Brownsville Revival in Pensacola, Florida. They both graduated from our Bible school and then joined us in 2003 to help launch a church in the Dallas area. For over a decade, I have had the privilege of laboring alongside him. His character has been tested and he has been found faithful. He is extremely gifted and carries a powerful anointing to minister the Word to this generation. What thrills me even more is that he's a man of integrity who walks in the fear of the Lord.

Daniel has preached in conferences throughout the United States and has appeared on both TBN and GodTV. He founded one of the most powerful youth events that airs regularly around the world. It is the best, period! The Collision Youth Conference continues to draw young people and leaders from around the nation. Daniel is committed to imparting the Truth into the hearts of all who attend. The results have been amazing.

Daniel delivers a clear, uncompromising presentation of the Gospel, gives compelling altar calls, and allows the Spirit of God to move when he ministers. In this day when there's such a mixture and unclear sound coming from so many pulpits, he is a breath of fresh air and boldly communicates the Truth in a spirit of love.

Introduction

My life was forever changed in an area no larger than three square feet. I could take you to the exact spot it happened. It was in a church just outside of Charleston, South Carolina. It was there that I had a genuine encounter with God. I don't remember much about that weekend. I can't tell you the message that was preached. I don't even know the name of the evangelist who preached it. I just remember that moment when I became alive in God, and He became real to me. Before then I didn't know such a relationship with the divine was even possible.

It was spring break of '96. I was finishing up my first year at Clemson University. I had joined up with several friends who were attending a youth conference in the lower part of the state. Church was something I had always grown up around, but now as I was in college it had taken a backseat to other pursuits.

It just wasn't relevant anymore. Church was something I did out of religious tradition, but it wasn't real to me. I had decided after eighteen years of following the path set for me by my parents it was time to chart my own course. I was my own man now and ready to experience all the world had to offer.

I would still attend church and I certainly looked the part whenever I entered the doors. I knew how to put on a good show and had many fooled. However, the friends I hung out with knew there was another side. I was a backsliding, lukewarm, apathetic, and complacent Christian. I knew a lot about God, but I didn't really know Him.

Sunday morning I'd be in church with hands lifted in worship. I would even volunteer to help throughout the week. However, come Friday you might find me lakeside by a fire drinking alcohol we had just stolen from a grocery store. I was just a sinner who was pretty good at pretending to be a saint. It was a life of hypocrisy.

This was how I arrived to the conference that day: a lost sinner, with a saintly facade. I didn't come for the service—I came for my friends. I loved the lower part of the state and wanted to be around the coast. Attending the conference was just an excuse to be there.

I sat on the back row through the entire service. There wasn't another seat farther from that pulpit. The evangelist had come from a revival that was taking place in Pensacola, Florida. He was fired up about what God had done in him. I don't remember his message, but I do remember he preached for over an hour before giving an altar call that lasted another forty-five minutes.

I remember it because I fought that appeal all forty-five of those minutes. I stood with my hands firmly grasping the seat in front of me. Nothing could move me. This evangelist was not going to get me out of my seat. As he pushed harder and harder I just dug in deeper and deeper.

Nearly every person in the place filled the altar—everyone but me. He finally ended the altar call. I breathed a sigh of relief and let go of the seat in front of me. My knuckles were white from clinching that seat for so long.

I stood waiting for the dismissal of the service, but there wasn't one. The evangelist simply said to the few stragglers left in the auditorium, "I want to open the altars for anyone who wants to get closer to God."

I don't know why I responded, but I did. Looking back, I believe it was because I let my guard down after having fought so hard before. The Holy Spirit saw an opening, and He graciously tugged at my heart.

I left the seat that minutes earlier I was so fastened to and walked all the way down to the altar area of the church. I stood there, alone. I could already tell something was beginning to happen to me. I lifted my hands and closed my eyes. After all, that's what you do when you're going after God, right?

Suddenly I was completely overwhelmed by the presence of the Lord. He came to me at that altar and when He did I was completely weakened. All the strength left my body and I could no longer stand. I collapsed to the ground and was unable to move.

I didn't know what to think at the time. When things like this would happen in church, I made fun of it. I didn't believe it. Now here I am lying on the ground, unable to move. No one had prayed for me, no one had pushed me down. I simply could not stand, nor could I move.

That is when it happened. I heard His voice; His beautiful, still, small voice. Jesus began speaking to me concerning His plans and purposes for my life. He spoke of my calling and about His heart for the young people at our church. He said revival was coming!

This was the first time I had ever really listened to Him. Looking back now I can see that He was always speaking. I just wasn't listening. Now my ears were attentive to His voice and that morning I surrendered my life to Him. I came to church one way, but left another. The young man that entered the building wasn't the same one who exited. Everything was different.

I had no clue just how much had changed; at least not right away. I didn't say much on the ride home. I was still processing what had happened and I certainly wasn't prepared for what was about to happen.

Every morning for two weeks the Lord would wake me up at five in the morning. That same still, small voice that I heard at the altar would clearly be speaking. I would spend two hours in prayer with the Lord. He was teaching me to listen. I began to write down what I heard Him say. I began to hunger deeply for His word. I couldn't stop reading my Bible.

I called my pastor and asked if we could meet. We connected the following morning at a little breakfast house that was on the way to college. I shared with him what had taken place. I wasn't sure if I was losing my mind or if this was legitimate.

With tears in my eyes, I opened the notebook I had been writing in and asked him to take a look. Within a few minutes of reading, he was weeping as well. He asked that I share it with our students.

That following Sunday a revival began to break out among the teenagers within our church. For six months we experienced a sovereign move of the Spirit in which young men and women from all walks of life would come and experience the power and presence of God. The very things God had spoken to me in the altar of that church weeks earlier were now taking place.

There are moments in life that become pivot points in our journey. They come unexpectedly and forever alter the trajectory of our path. This was one of my major pivot points. Everything that has happened in my life these last two decades can be traced back to that encounter at the altar.

Is it possible you are on the verge of one of those pivot points within your own life? Nothing happens by accident. You are reading this book for a reason. My prayer for you is that these words will spark a fire within your spirit and cause you to turn your ears toward His voice.

God is not silent! He is speaking and has been speaking all along. Though we may hear Him, we aren't always listening. When we do listen, it is often for brief periods. Few find that place of constant communion with the Lord. This is where Jesus lived—always attentive to His Father's voice. Thankfully this is not exclusive to Jesus. He made it clear this place of communion with God is available to any who would seek it out.

The Lord has been at work in you, longer than you realize, to make you receptive to His word. His desire has always been to be in relationship with you. There is a secret to cultivating this receptiveness in your life. It simply requires you yielding to His work.

Just as I stopped fighting Him on that back row of the church and finally surrendered, it's time to let go and let His Spirit loose within you.

If you have never surrendered your life to Jesus, why waste another second? The Bible makes it clear that all of us have sinned and fallen short of the glory of God. No one is good enough to stand before a perfect God. We are all guilty of sin.

God's Word also says that the wages of sin is death. There is a cost for sin and that price is death. All those who have not put their faith in Jesus will perish. The bad news is if you do not know Jesus, you are on your way to hell.

The good news is there is a way out. John 3:16 says, *"For God so loved the world that He gave His only begotten son, that whosoever believes in Him should not perish but have eternal life."*

You can invite Jesus into your life right now. The Bible says that if we believe in our heart and confess with our mouth that Jesus is Lord then we shall be saved. If you have never asked Jesus into your life, would you do so now? Pray this prayer with me:

> *Jesus, I believe You are the Son of God. I believe You died upon the cross for my sins and I believe that You rose from the dead. I repent of my sins and ask for Your forgiveness. Wash me, cleanse me, and make me new just like You. I give myself to You. Come live Your life in me. Be my Lord, my Savior, and my very best friend. In Your name I pray. Amen!*

Chapter One

Are You Listening?

We are all masters at hearing but not listening...some better than others.

"After this, Jesus traveled about from one town and village to another, proclaiming the good news of the kingdom of God. The Twelve were with him..."

"While a large crowd was gathering and people were coming to Jesus from town after town, He told this parable: 'A farmer went out to sow his seed. As he was scattering the seed, some fell along the path; it was trampled on, and the birds of the air ate it up. Some fell on rock, and when it came up, the plants withered because they had no moisture. Other seed fell among thorns, which grew up with it and choked the plants. Still other seed fell on good soil. It came up and yielded a crop, a hundred times more than was sown.'"

"When He said this, He called out, 'He who has ears to hear, let him hear.'"

—Luke 8:1-8, NIV

My wife tells me I have selective hearing. She's right. Jenna has accurately diagnosed a condition that I have had for quite some time. I'm not alone. Selective hearing is something most men are very familiar with. It is a skill we have honed for years until we have become masters of hearing, but not really listening. Let's face it, there are some things we are just more receptive to hearing than others.

For instance, as a husband I love to hear my wife tell me that she loves me. As a father I love to hear the sound of my little boy's feet running across the floors. I love the way he draws out my name with excitement every time he sees me. He says, "Da-Deeee" and follows it with, "Wove-ew!" Others may not understand what he is saying, but to me it is truly music to my ears.

I was very receptive to my little girl's first words. They were *Da-Da* and she spoke them on Mother's Day, into a microphone in front of three hundred people. I loved it! That was an amazing Mother's Day gift.

I love to hear someone tell me, "You're doing a good job." Who doesn't like to hear an *atta boy* or *way to go*? Recognition for work well done is always appreciated. All of us are receptive to these affirming statements.

As a preacher I love to hear the applause and amens from an audience. It lets you know that your words are connecting and that people are listening...or at least pretending to. Nothing is more discouraging than to be ministering God's word with great boldness and passion to a congregation of stoic saints silently sitting in their seats with blank stares.

The great revivalist Leonard Ravenhill often remarked that he hadn't raised the dead yet, but he preached to them all the time. I know, I've been to that church before. You arrive praying for revival, but quickly start interceding for resurrection. Finally you realize what they really need is to be laid to rest.

Just as there are things that I am receptive to hearing, there are a lot of things that I am not. I mentioned all the wonderful things I love to hear from my children, like the sound of my son's little feet on the floor. I didn't mention that oftentimes those footsteps are followed by loud crashes and clashes as he runs full speed into a wall. It's funny for a second—then come the screams. I am amazed at the sheer volume that such a little person is capable of producing. How can that precious little angelic face let out a scream that sounds like it originated from somewhere far, far from Heaven? There have been a few times I have wondered if I should lay hands on him and pray for deliverance.

I don't like to hear babies crying—not in restaurants and especially not on planes, where there is no chance to escape. I thought being a parent would make me more tolerant of their screams. I was wrong! I am convinced the most annoying sound on planet earth to the human ear has to be the sustained cries of an infant. God wisely designed it that way so that no parent could ignore the needs of his or her baby.

When our first child was born we woke up every few hours to feed her just as much for our sanity as for her sake. We'd slap one another in the middle of the night and say, "The baby is crying," and this wasn't our way of stating the obvious. It was parent code for, "it's your turn to take care of her and silence the noise so I can sleep."

Thankfully I learned to exercise my talent for selective hearing as babies two and three came into the world. Jenna marveled in disbelief how her husband, who usually wakes up at the slightest of sounds, could suddenly sleep through their cries. Selective hearing can be quite useful.

I don't want to hear *oops* when I am at the dentist sitting in his chair with those instruments of torture protruding from my mouth. I don't want to hear a doctor say, "I've never seen anything like that before." I'm not receptive to these things!

When I was a kid I didn't want to hear my dad say, "This is going to hurt me more than it hurts you." One time I thought it would be a good idea to respond back, "If that's true then why don't we trade places?" I only did that once, as it didn't work out for me as well as I'd hoped.

Another thing I am not receptive to is the word *but*. Especially when it comes after a word of encouragement. This is the telltale sign you are about to be *sandwiched*. Sandwiching is when you "need to talk" to someone about something you know they will not be receptive to, so you take the subject and sandwich it between two slices of something sweet.

The technique is simple and comes naturally for most of us. First, you say something to soften up the person you need to talk to. Next, you smack them with the rebuke. Last, you follow up the rebuke with something sweet.

It's a tactic parents have tried unsuccessfully for generations when it comes to getting their kids to eat something good for them. "A spoonful of sugar helps the medicine go down" sounds great in a song, but often fails in the Norris household. Jenna will take a spoonful of medicine and place whipped cream on top. Our child's eyes light up when they see it. They start to salivate over what seems to be a tasty treat, then their eyes start to tear up as they spit it out in disgust, giving you that "how could you betray me" stare afterward.

This is exactly what it feels like to be sandwiched. Let me give you an example of a typical act of sandwiching at church. A dear precious saint will come to me saying, "Pastor, I really need to talk to you..." My guard goes up every time I hear someone say, "I need to talk to you." No one ever "needs" to talk to me about something good. I pray for the day that someone would "need to talk to me" about donating a million dollars to reach souls all over the world! Unfortunately those are not the conversations I have following these words.

I try my best to resist that sense for self-preservation and instinct to run for cover. Graciously I respond, "What can I do for you?" They then start to sandwich what they need to say with what they think I want to hear.

"Pastor, you are really doing a great job and that message you just preached really ministered to me...."

I brace myself because I hear it coming, and can even see them working toward getting it out as if they feel there is a proper timing in releasing the next part.

"We absolutely love you."

Here it comes.

"But..."

And that *but* is followed up with how they feel you're not doing a good job, how the message was all wrong, and how I could better minister to their family. Often they provide an example of how their previous pastor did things and how I could learn a thing or two from him.

Isn't it amazing how so much can change because of that one three-letter word? It came in and erased all the wonderful things they just said, leaving me with the sting of that rebuke. Thankfully they don't linger here too long. To complete the sandwich they then let me know they are praying for me. After all, everything sounds spiritual when we mention prayer, doesn't it?

Grammatically we use *but* as a contrasting conjunction. It is a word that connects two statements that are different from one another. It creates a line of separation within the sentence that changes everything.

There are times the result of this conjunction is a very good thing. For instance, in Genesis chapter six, God is set to destroy the entire earth because the wickedness of mankind. When all hope seems lost and the world is coming to an end, verse eight says, "***But** Noah found grace in the eyes of the Lord*" (Genesis 6:8). That little three-letter word changed everything for humanity because Noah found favor in God's eyes.

Peter wrote, "*The Lord is not slack concerning His promise, as some count slackness, but is longsuffering toward us, not willing that any should perish*" (2 Peter 3:9).

We were lost and perishing, *but* because the Lord is patient with us, He gives us time to repent. What a great word! Once again it changes everything in our favor if we simply repent.

Search the scriptures and you'll find *but* nearly four thousand times. I thank God for each of those. Some come as words of warning and others as words of hope. They tell us that we were lost, alone, and dead within our sin and that we deserved punishment *but* God loved us! He makes the path clear and gives us everything we need to succeed. We make the decision where we find ourselves on that line of separation.

We find another example of this in Luke. Jesus says, "*The knowledge of the secrets of the kingdom of God has been given to you, **but** to others I speak in parables, so that, 'though seeing, they may not see; though hearing, they may not understand'*" (Luke 8:10, NIV).

Jesus makes it clear that there are two groups of people. Those who will receive the knowledge of the secrets of the kingdom and those who will not. Again we make the decision as to which side of that statement we will live.

Do you have ears to hear? This is the question Jesus asks. He calls out in a loud voice to the multitude gathered that day and says, "Listen!" He then shares a powerful parable that offers a pivotal principle in the kingdom of God. He then asks, "Did you hear what I said?"

Jesus was the greatest of communicators. He was attentive to the receptiveness of the multitude that had gathered around Him that day. He knew they were hearing, but not listening. Though they had the ears to hear, they chose not to listen.

They were content to simply enjoy His presence and experience the miracles. Some marveled at His command of scripture, but no one allowed the truth He shared to penetrate beyond the surface and bring a transformation in their lives. They came, they saw, they heard, and they left no different than they arrived. What a shame.

That day Jesus offered up the key to discovering a rich and productive relationship with the Lord. Everyone who heard Him could have experienced a seismic shift in their life that would have forever changed them, but they were not listening. The same could be said of us. That same key is waiting to be discovered by those who would read it and heed it.

How much are we like this multitude? Far too many rely too heavily on the experience of a weekend service at church. They come and enjoy the presence of God in the sanctuary; they celebrate the testimonies of His power or experience a miracle themselves. They praise the preacher and enjoy his messages—some even take notes. Then they leave the same way they came. If your spiritual life hasn't changed in a noticeable way over the years, then your religious activities aren't making a difference. You're just going through the motions but not actually moving anywhere.

The crowds missed it but the disciples didn't. They knew enough to dig a little deeper. They had followed Jesus for months and could tell that there was something here they had to catch. They came to Him privately and asked, "What does this parable mean?"

Jesus answers, "*The knowledge of the secrets of the kingdom of God has been given to you, but to others I speak in parables, so that, 'though seeing, they may not see; though hearing, they may not understand*'" (Luke 8:10, NIV).

He spoke in a parable and painted a clear picture with His words that even a child could understand. However, they didn't listen. They missed it, *but* for His disciples the secrets of the kingdom of Heaven are available. They are already ours if we will be attentive and learn to listen.

Those who desire to discover the secrets of God's kingdom need to learn to be like the disciples and find that secret place with Jesus where we can hear His voice and see the truth of His words. Your devotional life is the single most important part of your life. The person who fails here fails everywhere. No amount of church attendance or other religious activities will be able to replenish the deficit created by a life where prayer is absent. It's a vital key to learning to listen.

My friend, we cannot miss this. We are all masters at hearing but not listening; some better than others. However, the mysteries and secrets of God's kingdom are reserved for those with ears to hear. You and I are about to embark on a journey into a life in the Spirit that you never knew was possible. A life in which your ears are in tune with the voice of Heaven, always listening to what God is speaking—and trust me, God is speaking.

This journey for me began twenty years ago and I am still discovering more and more every day. What I have learned thus far in listening to the voice of God is something I want to share with you because I believe it will change your life. Of all the things that one could be receptive to, His voice should be on the top of the list.

SEEING THE FULLNESS OF HIS GLORY

When Jesus said, "*Seeing they may not see, and hearing they may not understand*", He was quoting from Isaiah 6, which begins by saying:

> "*In the year that King Uzziah died, I saw the Lord sitting on a throne, high and lifted up, and the train of His robe filled the temple. Above it stood seraphim; each one had six wings: with two he covered his face, with two he covered his feet, and with two he flew. And one cried to another and said: 'Holy, holy, holy is the Lord of hosts; the whole earth is full of His glory!'*" (Isaiah 6:1-3).

Notice how Isaiah dates his vision. He says, "*In the year that King Uzziah died.*" This was more than just marking the time of the vision—it marked the setting for it as well. This was one of those "remember where you were when" moments. A great king had died and a nation was in mourning.

We have all experienced such times. Though we are far removed from the date of September 11, 2001, I still remember where I was when I heard that terrorists had attacked our nation. I was on my knees in prayer during chapel at Bible school. I remember the exact spot I was kneeling and what I was wearing. I'll never forget that moment.

Many referred to 9/11 as our generation's Pearl Harbor. My grandparents could tell you exactly where they were and what they were doing on December 7, 1941, when they first heard of the Japanese bombing of Pearl Harbor. These days that live in infamy forever mark our lives as time stamps that altered our course in some way.

For Isaiah, this was one of those moments. He remembers where he was when he heard the news break that the king had died. His heart was heavy as he began to grieve. This was not a time of celebration. Yet in the midst of the sadness, Isaiah has a revelation. He says, *"In the year the king died, I saw the Lord."*

Let that go through you. You may be currently facing the worst ordeal of your life. You may feel like catastrophe is all around you. You may wonder how you are going to make it. Listen to these words: in your darkest hour, you too can see the Lord.

I can't help but notice that for Isaiah to see the Lord something had to die. What has been standing between you and Jesus? What needs to die in order for your eyes to be opened? The Lord is gracious enough to allow the kings in our lives to die so that He alone can sit upon the throne of our hearts. Every trial and test you face is an opportunity to move obstacles out of your path and see a fresh vision of the Lord. The trial you are currently engaged in can reveal the Lord if you simply open your eyes and see.

This vision changes Isaiah's life. As one thing was coming to an end, something brand new was about to take place in the prophet's life. He saw the Lord high and lifted up. He heard the thunderous sound of the angels that encircled around the throne. Isaiah said that as they hid their faces they exclaimed, *"Holy, holy, holy is the Lord God Almighty! The whole earth is filled with His glory."*

Look at what they are saying. Yes, they declared the holiness of God, but listen further—they also said, *"The whole earth is filled with His glory."*

What wonderful news that had to be for the prophet. The earth is *filled* with His glory! It hadn't seemed that way for Isaiah. His king had passed away and all hope was lost. The people wondered where God was in the midst of all the chaos. From the perspective of the earth things didn't seem so glorious.

Yet through an act of God's grace Isaiah is ushered up to Heaven to obtain a heavenly perspective. From the vantage point of the kingdom the angels showed Isaiah something he couldn't see before. The earth is filled with the glory of God.

When we are in the depths of our pit it is hard to see anything else but the walls. Looking ahead is impossible. God doesn't see things the way we do. His view is high above our problems. What seems like a chasm to us is not even a ditch to Him! What seems like an insurmountable mountain to us is not even a hill for our God!

You may be in the midst of your darkest hour or facing the greatest challenge of your life. Maybe you've suffered a tremendous loss. If you only see things from the perspective of this planet you will miss the great and glorious thing that God is doing in the midst of that very situation. Open your eyes and hear with your ears and you will discover that right now, your situation is filled with the glory of God. He is here with you in the midst of the circumstance.

The same is true for those who say times are good. For you everything may be fine and you've got nothing to worry about. Heed this word of caution. The best of times can often be more dangerous to us than the worst of times. When the sailing is smooth, we get lax at the wheel. Tough times often cause us to instinctively call out to God. Good times often cause us to slowly drift away.

Remember in the good times and the bad times He is still God. He is unmoved and unchanged by our present situations. If we will invite Him to give us His perspective on our present position, we will usher ourselves into the glory that is all about us, yet we somehow continue to miss.

God reveals to His prophet, "Yes Isaiah, the king has died, but the earth is still full of my glory! I am still here in the midst of your mess. Though an earthly king has stepped off his throne, your eternal king still occupies His."

If that was true in Isaiah's day, how much more so now? Jesus has come, the kingdom of God is here. Truly the earth is now full of His glory. Can you see it? Do you see His glory in your home, work, school? Did you see it throughout your day or are you missing it? It is so easy to have eyes to see and ears to hear, yet we miss what is plainly in front of us.

Isaiah's eyes were now open. His ears were now attentive. In the year King Uzziah died, Isaiah finally saw the Lord! He would never be the same.

The Lord commissions the prophet to go and speak to the people on His behalf, but He tells him that the people will not listen. He said, *"Go, and tell this people: 'Keep on hearing, but do not understand; keep on seeing, but do not perceive'. Make the heart of this people dull, and their ears heavy, and shut their eyes; lest they see with their eyes, and hear with their ears, and understand with their heart, and return and be healed."* (Isaiah 6:9-10).

Isaiah's life has been changed, but that will not be the case for his audience. He is forewarned that his mission will seem unsuccessful from an earthly perspective. The people's eyes will be dulled and their ears will be closed to the words God places in the prophet's mouth. Isaiah's eyes and ears are open, but the eyes and ears of the nation will be shut. They will not listen, nor will they be receptive to the truth. This is unfortunate, because if they could understand it with their whole hearts they'd turn back to the Lord and be healed.

Notice this is the passage that Jesus pointed to when speaking to His disciples. He said, "*The knowledge of the secrets of the kingdom are now fully disclosed to those who have ears to hear*". Many will miss out on what is clearly revealed, even though they see it, even though they hear it. They will miss it.

But those who have eyes to see and ears to hear and those who have hearts that understand will turn and be healed. So much can change with that three-lettered word.

The answer to every situation you face and the way to live your life to the fullest is found in your ability to hear. Learning to see and hear the secrets of His kingdom is the key to accomplishing the God-sized dreams that reside within you. This is what I mean by *Receptivity.*

How might your life change if you choose to disengage the selective hearing we are so naturally prone to and begin actively listening to what the Spirit is saying at this very moment?

Jesus called out, "Let him who has ears to hear, let him hear!" Are you ready to listen?

> *Lord You opened the eyes of the blind and the ears of the deaf. I ask You to do that in me. I want to see You and Your glory here on earth. I want to hear Your voice and listen to Your words. Lord I have ears to hear; I am ready to listen.*

Chapter Two

The Selfless Sower

He has graciously and generously spoken His word but are we really listening?

"Listen! A farmer went out to sow his seed. As he was scattering..."
—MARK 4:3, NIV

Nestled into the foothills of the Blue Ridge Mountains in South Carolina is a little fourteen-acre farm that I once called home. This homestead belonged to my grandfather, who was a part-time farmer and a full-time preacher. He was a godly and gracious man who gave his sons portions of his property to raise their own families. It was a blessing to have such a peaceful place to grow up and even more to have such a spiritual upbringing.

Most mornings you would see my grandfather, who we affectionately called Pop, out in the fields dressed in his blue coveralls, riding atop an old 1954 Ford Jubilee tractor. That tractor was a work of art, sculpted and styled like the art-deco vehicles of the era with bold lines and big curves. It was hard to miss out in the field as the long hood of the tractor sat like a white shroud atop its bright red body. I can still hear the distinct chime of that four-cylinder engine and smell the aroma of the hydraulics mixed with the fumes from the exhaust.

I loved riding in Pop's lap while he managed that powerful beast with an ease that only comes after decades of practice. He had spent countless hours on the back of that tractor working the fields throughout the years. Every season had a different need and each need required a different tool. The lot behind the barn was littered with those tools. There were mowers, rakers, tillers, and scrapers along with various plows. All had different functions yet fulfilled the same purpose—soil preparation.

As spring approached, Pop would begin the tedious but important process of preparing the soil. He would mow, rake, and scrape the field to remove the persistent weeds and tall grass that had grown during the colder months. Next he would attach the tiller to that old Ford and start to break up the ground that had been left to fallow during the winter. The tiller had a dozen large blades that would rip and tear into the earth, loosening the dirt. Pop took a great amount of time to get the soil ready. He'd turn it over again and again, pulling out the weeds and removing the rocks that had been pulled up. It struck me that every year there were always new rocks. I thought sooner or later the rocks had to come to an end, but every new season seemed to bring a few more to the surface.

Once he felt the soil was to his satisfaction he would begin to plow the field, creating neatly lined furrows that were so perfect you would think he had followed a guide.

The dirt smelled rich and ran freely between your fingers. It was so loose the plow would move through it like a comb parting hair.

It took a great deal of time to get the field properly prepared and ready to be sown. This was an important step that couldn't be overlooked. The preparation beforehand was necessary to ensure the quality of the harvest later on.

Now it was time to sow the seed and Pop was meticulous about where each one went. Every seed had its proper place within the furrow and was placed with care by hand. Nothing was wasted. He taught me that there was nothing more precious than the seed. He would say, "If we did our job right preparing the soil, the seed would do its job of producing the fruit."

That lesson is true, not just in the garden but in our lives as well. Growing up on a farm gives you a different perspective of this parable of the sower. I imagine many in the multitude that had gathered along the shoreline to hear Jesus had to have had the same reaction I did the first time I read this parable. In a Middle Eastern culture where agriculture is the heart of their community Jesus begins to share a parable to illustrate the kingdom of God by painting the picture of a sower unlike any they had ever seen—a seemingly foolish one.

This sower was indiscriminate about where his seed fell. He simply reached into his sack of seeds and cast them wide as he walked. They fell upon the path, the rocks, the thorns, and eventually some found its way upon good soil. The immediacy that Jesus shares the fate of each seed seems to communicate the fact that even the sower knew the outcome for each seed before he threw it, yet he threw it anyway.

Surely the listeners would have reacted to the foolishness of a sower who would so carelessly scatter his seed. Did he not understand how precious the seed was? Was he not concerned about the fruit? Was he just wasting his time? Who is this fool?

The idea that my grandfather would ever take a seed and sow it outside the garden would never have crossed his mind. He wouldn't scatter seed on his concrete driveway—it would be wasted there. Nor would he take his seed and throw it onto the gravel road leading up to the farm. There is no way it would survive. Not once did I ever see him pour out seed on the outer edges of the garden in the grass where the weeds would soon be springing up.

He was a master gardener, and every gardener knows you do not waste your seed. It's too precious. If he did his job right, only then could the seed do its job!

Did Jesus not understand what He was talking about? Was there something to this story that everyone was missing? Why is it no one in the crowd stopped Jesus to ask Him what He meant?

Jesus wrapped up this short parable the way He began, with an exclamation. He starts the parable saying, "Listen!" and finishes by raising His voice and saying, "Let he who has ears to hear, let him hear!"

Any parent of a young child understands exactly what Jesus was doing. When I need to communicate something important to my seven-year-old daughter or two-year-old son, I make eye contact with them and say, "Listen to me." It's not until they look at me that I share what I need them to know. Then I follow up with, "Do you understand?"

Communicating with a two-year-old is often like trying to speak to someone who doesn't know your language. It is funny to watch someone talk slow and loud in English to a non-English-speaking individual as if that is going to help. They just stare back, smile, and nod. This is often how I feel when trying to talk to my son.

He doesn't enjoy being verbally corrected. When he does something wrong, like pushing his sister or hitting his brother over the head with a toy hammer, he will immediately put himself in time-out when I call his name. He runs over to the corner while saying, "Sorry." It's cute—he would rather discipline himself than have someone else do it. I call him over to me, get down on my knees, and look him in the eyes. He refuses to look at me. Even when I gently place my hands on that cute little face and point it toward me, he will not make eye contact. He's done this since he was nine months old. I suppose he thinks, "If I can't see you, I can't hear you either." I know that until he's looking at me, he's not really listening.

Jesus asks for the multitude's undivided attention, "Listen!" He then shares a powerful truth of God's kingdom and follows it up with, "Did you really hear what I said?"

Sadly the answer that day was no. Both the crowd and the disciples listened to the parable—neither understood it. It didn't make sense to them. The crowds departed that day with a story they didn't understand. However, the disciples began to hunger for more.

Later that evening they came to Jesus in private and asked, "What did you mean with this parable?" They obviously realized that they had missed the significance. However, unlike the crowd that left without understanding, they came to Jesus to get it. It was those who were closest to Jesus who were not content to just let the parable remain a story—they wanted to know the truth contained within it.

Notice the setting in which they came to Jesus: in private. There are things that you will never hear from the Lord if you choose to remain content to simply receive everything from someone else. You may attend a great church, have a great library of books, or listen to the best of preachers, but there is no substitute for finding some alone time with Jesus to ask Him for the deeper things that are not discussed in the midst of multitudes!

It's in this setting that Jesus begins to uncover His secrets. The Lord's precious secrets are only revealed in private settings! He answers the disciples, *"The knowledge of the secrets of the kingdom of God has been given to you, but to others I speak in parables."*

I will never forget sitting in the office of my friend and mentor evangelist Steve Hill. This mighty man of God had been used to usher in the longest running revival America had ever seen—a revival that started on Father's Day of 1995 and continued for five straight years. Over four million people visited the revival and were forever changed. Steve was mentored by another great revivalist named Leonard Ravenhill who wrote the classic book *Why Revival Tarries.* I sat across the desk from Steve as he shared with me various stories about what it was like to sit with Ravenhill. I couldn't help but be humbled by the fact that here I sat across from Steve, very much like Steve sat across from Ravenhill decades earlier.

The tone of Steve's voice changed as he began to share this story. His shift in tone shifted the atmosphere of the room. I leaned in knowing that what Steve was about to share was too precious to be missed. He said, "I was sitting across from Leonard in his office when he called me up out of my seat and asked me to come closer." Steve stood up and walked to Ravenhill's side, but Leonard called him even closer. Steve leaned over to where the two now were face to face. Leonard still called him closer. Steve turned his head—as he brought his ear closer to Ravenhill's mouth, Ravenhill whispered,

"Closer." At this point Steve moved in as close as possible. He could feel Leonard's breath against his ear. It was uncomfortably close, but it was the position he had to be in to hear the next words that came from Ravenhill's mouth.

Leonard said with a soft reverence, "Steve, the Lord has secrets. But He only whispers them. You have to live close enough to God that you can hear His gentle whispers."

I sat back in my chair. There was now an awe in the room as if we had left the confines of this planet and been ushered into the Lord's presence. With tears in his eyes, Steve began to call upon the Lord. "Jesus we want to hear your gentle whispers. We want to live so close to you that we can hear that still small voice. Draw us in, Jesus."

I cherish that story, and even more I've taken that moment to heart. It has produced a deep longing within me to know Christ more intimately. I am willing to be discomforted if necessary to find that position that puts my ear in front of his lips. I long for those private settings where His precious secrets are unearthed.

Jesus said to those close to Him, *"The knowledge of the secrets of the kingdom of God has been given to you."* Oh what blessedness to know His secrets and to know that He has given them to those who position themselves close to Him!

Jesus continues, *"To others I speak in parables, so that, 'though seeing, they may not see; though hearing, they may not understand'"* (Luke 8:10 NIV). He spoke in a parable and painted a clear picture with His words, but those on the outside didn't understand it.

Thankfully we are not on the outside. The Lord has brought us close to Himself and given us access to the secrets of the kingdom contained within His words. It is unfortunate that many will choose to miss it. They have eyes to see and ears to hear, but not you! These secrets are yours. The parable may have satisfied the curiosity of the crowd, but the true disciple is compelled to dive deeper.

Mark records Jesus saying, *"but to those who are outside, all things come in parables"* (Mark 4:11, NIV). Yes, Jesus called the multitude who gathered earlier that day outsiders. They came to see and hear Jesus and left content with just the experience. They came from the outside and chose to remain on the outside.

No one has to remain outside. Though the door to His kingdom is narrow—that gate is swung wide open to whosoever would enter. Jesus has not barred anyone from coming in—in fact, He's enabled them to do so. The difference is in who has the ears to truly hear His invitation.

Consider the next statement Jesus makes. *"Don't you understand this parable? How then will you understand any parable?"* (Mark 4:13, NIV). For years I misunderstood this parable. I was taught it was solely a passage pertaining to evangelism. The evangelist is presented as the sower and the seed as the Gospel. Though that is a great illustration to draw from the parable there is so much more to discover.

Notice that Jesus is now speaking only to His disciples. Earlier the parable was spoken to the people, but this is directed at those closest to Him. The truth of this parable wasn't just about the lost, but even more for those who had been found.

Jesus asks, *"Don't you understand?"* Like a good teacher He stops to make sure His students understands the elementary things before pursuing greater things. He then emphasizes that if you can't see this, you'll miss everything else from this point on.

You can see here how Jesus is truly patient and selfless toward us. He is willing to take the time that is necessary to work with us until we can understand His truth. We can follow the example set by the disciples. When you see something or hear something you do not understand or that sparks your curiosity take it to Him in prayer and watch as the Holy Spirit brings light to what was previously veiled. He has not left us alone to figure it out—He promised to give us His spirit to *"teach you all things, and bring to your remembrance all things"* that He said (John 14:26).

The fact that Jesus's explanation of the parable is captured in three of the Gospels is worth noting. Out of the forty-six parables in the Gospels, most are offered with no interpretation. This is the only one that receives a complete explanation. Why? It is the parable of parables. It contains the key that unlocks not only the other parables, but the word of God itself.

That key is now in the door. Are you ready to enter?

The Seed of His Word

> *"This is the meaning of the parable: The seed is the word of God."* (Luke 8:11)

The seed is the word of God. John's first chapter eloquently tells us that Jesus Christ is the word made flesh. Jesus is both the word and the seed. This is a parallel that He clearly makes Himself when He says, *"Unless a grain of wheat falls into the ground and dies, it remains alone; but if it dies, it produces much grain"* (John 12:24).

If Jesus is the seed, then the sower can only be the Father who chose to sow His son into humanity (a thought I am continually in awe of). God selflessly gave His Son to a world that He knew would not receive Him. *"He came to that which was His own, but His own received Him not"* (John 1:11). God graciously and generously cast His Son onto the hard, rocky, and thorny ground. Did He do so in vain? Consider this psalm:

> *Those who sow in tears shall reap in joy. He who continually goes forth weeping, bearing seed for sowing, shall doubtless come again with rejoicing, bringing his sheaves with him* (Psalm 126:5-6).

The *"seed for sowing"* that the sower bears is *"precious seed"* as the King James calls it. How precious indeed! This word literally means "seed-draught." The picture created is that of seed that is drawn out of the seed box to be cast upon the field.

The image painted by the psalmist is of a sower who steps out into the field and upon seeing the dry, parched land begins to weep. There is nothing to reassure him that the soil is fertile, yet he still must sow the precious seed. With a river of tears he casts his seed upon dry ground. The sower *"continually goes forth."* There is no end to the sowing nor is there an end to the weeping. He sows in such a way in the hope that one day there will likewise be no end to the reaping.

The Father sent forth His Son, His only Son, into the world. God drew Him out of Himself in order to sow Him into fallen humanity. This was God's precious word and that word became flesh. The word was seed that was selflessly cast upon the earth's dry ground. Jesus, like His Father, drew that seed out from Himself and continually did so until every last seed was fully poured out. He came forth weeping, but did so willingly because of the *"joy set before Him"* (Hebrews 12:2), knowing that one day He would come again to gather a harvest greater than the tears.

The multitude heard it all wrong. He wasn't a foolish sower after all; He was a selfless sower. He didn't withhold the most precious of seed. His seed was not sown in vain. Not for me, not for you, and not for any who call upon His name. It wasn't sown in vain for the lost man or woman who keeps inching closer and closer to Hell, either. You see, when a man steps into eternity he will do so seeing the full extent God went to save him. On the Day of Judgment, God will show him the overwhelming seed that was poured out on his behalf. He will see every time he turned a deaf ear to the Gospel. He will be left with no doubt that God freely sowed His own Son into the earth so that he might be saved. Jesus was lifted up for all men to see, but we still make the choice to see.

Christ has done everything that He must do and could do so that you and I are without excuse. He is patient and long-suffering and does not want a single one of us to perish. So He went to the furthest extent and did everything necessary—all we have to do is open our ears to hear it!

In so many ways it doesn't make sense, but God never will to you and me. Our finite minds are incapable of grasping our infinite God. His thoughts are not our thoughts nor His ways our ways as Isaiah says:

> *"For My thoughts are not your thoughts, nor are your ways My ways," says the Lord. For as the heavens are higher than the earth, so are My ways higher than your ways, and My thoughts than your thoughts"* (Isaiah 55:8).

You and I will never fully understand how it works, but I am thankful that it always works. He sent forth His seed, His Son, into the world and it was not in vain! And it shall prosper in the lives of those who have attentive ears to hear what He is saying!

The Lord is no foolish farmer. He is a selfless sower who sows precious imperishable seed. Though it seems impossible nothing has been wasted for it will, in due season, accomplish what was intended. Isaiah continues, *"So shall My word be that goes forth from My mouth; it shall not return to Me void, but it shall accomplish what I please, and it shall prosper in the thing for which I sent it"* (Isaiah 55:11).

No seed is ever wasted in God's kingdom. It wasn't wasted in the years that I ran from Him. I constantly heard it calling me back. It certainly wasn't wasted in the years I have served Him either. It is bearing more and more fruit as the days go by. There wasn't a seed wasted on me.

Someone reading this right now is thinking of the seed you've sown that continues to tarry. You've held onto words and prayed prayers over friends and family. You have patiently waited on the breakthrough but it has not come yet. Listen to me. Trust the Seed!

His seed is imperishable. It will return to Him in the right season and the right time. Jenna and I worked with a young lady who was radically saved in our ministry. She was so on fire for the Lord, boldly sharing the Gospel with her friends and inviting them to church. Over time we watched that fire begin to fade until it seemed to be completely extinguished. Where she used to once boldly live for Jesus, she now just as boldly lived for the world. When she came by to see us, she would flaunt her prodigal lifestyle in front of us. We loved her just the same. I prayed asking Jesus where we failed her. He said to, Trust the seed.

It was five years later when I heard from her again. During that time I had wondered about her and prayed for her when she came to mind. She wrote us a message that I treasure to this day. She said, "Thank you for never giving up on me. You were the only ones in my life who cared enough to always tell me the truth even when it hurt. Now I am serving Jesus and involved with the ministries at my church. I am where I am today because of your faithfulness."

I cried when I read those words and remembered the Lord's words, "Trust the seed." I've now seen seed return that I sowed into many lives, some more than a decade ago. Pop was right: nothing is more precious than seed and the Lord's imperishable seed is most precious of all. Listen to me: trust the seed.

The selfless sower shows that God has overwhelmingly done everything on His end that He needs to do—the next step is completely ours. He has sown. Will we receive? He has revealed Himself. Will we look upon Him?

This parable is often referred to as the parable of the sower. Perhaps a more fitting title would be the parable of the soils. Jesus places the responsibility for the fruit not on the sower or the seed but upon the soil. The sower and the seed have done their part, now it is the soil's turn. The soil represents the hearer. If we do our job preparing the soil, the seed will do its job in producing the fruit. The responsibility now rests upon the hearer. Will we have ears to hear?

I'm thankful that my grandfather taught me how to work a field and sow seed. Not just in the garden, but in lives as well. Many days he would come in from working hours in the garden under the hot sun. He would take off his coveralls, take a shower, put on a suit, and head out to a different field. This time instead of sitting behind the wheel of his tractor he would be standing behind a pulpit under a tent or in a small country church. That night there might be a dozen people, but it didn't matter. Pop would begin to draw out of himself that same seed that was sown into him long ago. That precious seed that has been passed down generation to generation. That imperishable, incorruptible seed that was first sown at Calvary.

That night a man answers the altar call and receives Christ as Savior. The seed still works! Pop would lay hands on the sick, and they would get healed. The seed still works! He saw blind eyes open, limbs grow back, cancer fall off into his hands. The seed still works!

Several years ago I had the honor of preaching his funeral. During the funeral people came to know the Lord and people were healed. The seed still works!

Pop passed that seed on to my father, who passed it on to me. It is still bearing fruit in our lives. I've learned that God has secrets! He doesn't shout them, but He does selflessly sow them. His secrets are not available to a select few—they are fully disclosed to anyone who would choose to position themselves close enough to hear His voice. The door is open—you don't have to stay on the outside! Come on in.

> *Lord I thank You for so selflessly giving of Yourself for me. When I was lost and dead in my sin, still You came and died for me. You gave me life in exchange for the body of death I carried. You gave me hope when all was lost. You gave and You continue to give. Lord teach these ears to hear. Let the seed of Your word find fertile ground in me and may it return to You having accomplished all You desire.*

Chapter Three

Fallowed Ground

How religious and rebellious mindsets create faithless environments

"Those by the wayside are the ones who hear; then the devil comes and takes away the word out of their hearts, lest they should believe and be saved."
—Luke 8:12, NIV

I'M NOT LISTENING

You know the look, especially if you're a parent. You've likely faced it more times than you care to count. Your precious, sweet little princess has temporarily removed her angelic halo and borrowed a pitchfork. It often comes at the most inconvenient times when your potential for public embarrassment is all but guaranteed.

It may be aisle six of the grocery store or the foyer of your church just before checking them into the kids' church program. They've set their mind on something to the point that it has overwhelmed them. Apparently the four-year-old brain is only capable of holding a single thought and emotion at a time, and that emotion rarely comes with any moderation.

What has upset them seems trivial to you, but to them it has become the most important thing in the world, at least for the next few minutes. You know it's just a passing thought, totally impracticable, or just a sheer impossibility. You've sought to be polite and respectful, not drawing too much attention to them, yet for all your labor, the situation continues to escalate. They became unreasonable long before you realized it, and your attempts to have a rational dialogue have failed. That's a laughable thought, isn't it—a reasonable, rational dialogue with a four-year-old!

You've exhausted everything you've learned from the latest Proper Parenting 101 book you just read and now are embracing raw parental instinct. You raise your voice and call your child's name demanding their attention as you prepare to discipline them.

This is where the look comes into place. They throw the hip to one side, cock their head back, place those little hands over their ears, and begin to sing, "I can't hear you! I'm not listening! La-la, la-la, la lah."

I didn't teach them that song, nor can I recall a time they heard it from another child. It seems to have come preloaded in their internal playlist just waiting for me to find the right button to push that forces it out. It comes so naturally.

We tend to think of this scenario as one exclusive to children, but spiritually speaking we are all guilty of embracing it. This is the picture I imagine when I read Jesus's explanation of the hardened path.

Jesus explained, *"Those by the wayside are the ones who hear; then the devil comes and takes away the word out of their hearts"* (Luke 8:12, NIV). They are a hardened path that will not receive any seed. His words simply sit upon the top of the soil waiting to be carried away by the enemy.

A path is simply a hardened trail that has been worn into the earth from the constant footsteps of those who pass by. It's been walked upon so much that whatever life was there has been crushed and pounded into the ground until it has become dried out and hardened. This is what is known as fallow ground.

Fallow ground is uncultivated or hardened earth that is incapable of producing any fruit. It's infertile soil. Jesus compares this fallow soil to a person with fully closed ears. They are by the wayside, too hardened to receive the truth of his word. It will not penetrate because they are not listening. They can't hear—"La-la, la-la, la lah!"

The listening switch is in the off position. Though they may be looking at you and hearing the words, the message is simply passing straight through. They are not trying to actively hear and therefore the seed doesn't even have a chance to be planted into their hearts. It will never grow, let alone bear fruit. They are fully unreceptive.

Fallow ground within the heart keeps you from hearing the Lord's voice. Learning to be receptive requires dealing with hardened mindsets that close our ears. Every time you ignore the Lord's voice of conviction it grows fainter and fainter until it isn't heard at all. Some might falsely believe that the Lord's silence means He isn't speaking when the reality is they are no longer listening. Remember: the hardened path is the result of walking the same road over and over again. The wrong thoughts you've repeated within your heart and mind create a mindset that leaves you unreceptive. This is seen in the lives of two separate individuals.

THE HARD-HEARTED SINNER

The hardened path Jesus speaks of is often equated with the atheist, god-hater, or full-out heathen. We see a person who fully embraces their lifestyle of sin and has made a conscious decision to live their life in complete rebellion to God's truth. They don't want to hear anything!

I meet many people who are just like this. An unforgettable encounter came one evening in downtown Greenville, South Carolina, while doing street evangelism.

For those who have never ventured out of their comfort zone and stood like a "John the Baptist" on a street corner proclaiming the Gospel message, I encourage you to go out at least once. There is something about open-air preaching that brings the best and worst in people to the surface. A street preacher will create friction in an atmosphere of debauchery. His mere presence forces a reaction in the lives of the ungodly as well as the religious.

It's the weekend and sinners are out looking for a good time—they've come into the city to go to the bars or clubs and party, not listen to a preacher. They come from all walks of life. You're likely to meet the religious who will swing from one bar to the next on Saturday night and then still be in the sanctuary on Sunday morning. For the rest, church is the last thing on their minds. They will still be sleeping off last night's hangover long after the closing prayer is spoken from the pulpit.

As they make their way to the bars for a night of godlessness, they hear the godly message of truth being proclaimed from the preacher on the corner. Some are unmoved and pass the man of God by without a second thought. Some are angered at the audacity of the evangelist who would dare to confront their sins in the streets. Others are genuinely convicted by the words they hear.

It was not unusual to meet a young man and woman on the street who were just venturing out into the world. They had grown up in church and were raised in a godly home. Now they were out on their own and the temptation to step out of the religion of their youth was too great. However, as they made their way to the bar or club they were convicted by the loving yet bold truth they heard being shared from the street corner. It called them back to the Lord.

Today in the body of Christ there are many who feel that street preaching is out of date and out of place in the twenty-first century. They offer a list of excuses and justifications for their position, but I believe the primary reason is very simple. They are convicted by the boldness of a believer willing to go outside the four walls to do what they will not. That's how I used to feel when I would see the fiery street preacher. His red-hot words convicted me in my lukewarm lifestyle. I didn't like the way he made me feel so I challenged his validity.

We should be thankful for evangelists bold enough to go to the highways and byways to compel anyone willing to listen. They are often preaching to individuals who will never darken the door of a church but still need to hear the Gospel. I've heard far too many testimonies from lost sons and daughters who had truly bottomed out in life and that encounter with the evangelist out on the street became their turning point. It's because of these countless prodigals that are out on the streets that I say let the street preacher preach and send out more!

That night in the streets of Greenville, I was confronted by a man who could have been Goliath's little brother—he was smaller than the giant, but much larger than myself. He was dressed in all black. His clothes matched the darkness of his hair. There was a large skull on his shirt and around his neck was a silver pentagram. He came across the street shouting for us to shut up. I took the opportunity to speak directly to him, though he didn't want to hear a single word. The hate in his eyes and in his words was evident.

He cursed and screamed and then began to walk away. I called out to him, "Sir, one day you will stand before the God you deny. You will have to face Him."

He turned in the middle of the street and rushed my way shouting, "On that day, I will win." Then he swung at me with his open hand striking my face and throwing me to the ground. Rather than get mad, I suddenly was overwhelmed with the love of God for this man, and my heart broke. He was so unwilling to listen. He had ears to hear, but refused to hear. I don't know how his story ends—I hope that night might have softened his heart a bit for the next time he heard a seed of truth.

Sadly, *"the same heat that softens wax also hardens clay"* (Romans 7:1). Every time someone hears the Gospel message they make a decision to either move closer or further from God. It is absolutely impossible to hear the truth and leave unaffected. Those who reject it wear that hardened path deeper and deeper into their hearts.

It would not have mattered how long I preached to this man. He was not listening. There was no way the truth of God's word could find its way to his heart. There are multitudes of individuals like this. They have made a decision to close themselves to the Gospel and are unwilling to yield.

Their mind is made up. Therefore the word of God cannot penetrate their hearts.

Paul wrote, *"How, then, can they call on the one they have not believed in? And how can they believe in the one of whom they have not heard? And how can they hear without someone preaching to them"* (Romans 10:14)?

How can they hear without someone preaching to them? This is why the preacher is so important. That preacher may be a minister standing behind a pulpit or standing on a street corner. It's more likely the preacher is a coworker sitting across the table from a friend on a lunch break, a student sharing their testimony with a classmate, or a mother leading her little son to Jesus at the edge of his bed. Someone had to be the one to speak in order for someone else to hear. They opened their mouth and began to share the words of life. It's the way it works. Someone has to preach the truth.

Still, how can they believe, unless they hear? Not only does someone have to speak, someone has to listen. Unfortunately for the person on the wayside represented by the path, they refuse to hear. They've closed off their ears and will not listen to the truth. Since he will not hear, there is no way for him to believe.

Some might ask, "Then why preach to the closed minded?" Once again you can draw your attention to the selfless sower. He goes forth generously and graciously sowing precious seeds even upon the hardened hearts of a sinner who refuses to listen. In doing so, he demonstrates his love even for those who are hard to love. No seed is ever wasted, even upon those who refuse to hear.

That night on the street as the man walked away from me in anger, a crowd of people drew near. They had been watching from across the street. They saw a preacher who didn't cower in fear or get angry. They saw the compassion and instantly felt conviction concerning their own lives. One man refused to listen that night, but dozens more did hear. That night a mini revival broke out on the streets of Greenville. If you had simply judged that moment with the unreceptive man you would have called that night a failure, but you have to look at the full picture. I promise you, there wasn't a seed wasted!

THE HARDHEADED SAINT

Just as there are multitudes of hardened hearts walking the streets of your city, there are many of hardened heads sitting in the sanctuary as well. These are religious men and women who for one reason or another have put up walls and made up their minds with incorrect assumptions. They accept things as they see them and leave no room for correction. They are stuck in their status quo, reject the notion that there is more, and point the finger everywhere but at themselves. It doesn't matter what the truth really is because they refuse to hear it.

Right now you're likely thinking of a few individuals that fit this description. I'm not writing to them, but to you. Before you start dismissing this as someone else, take a moment to let the Holy Spirit speak to you. There are likely several things you've made your mind up about that are based on incorrect assumptions and opinions.

What is your view concerning divine healing, or spiritual gifts? Do you believe God still heals today or did miracles and the spiritual gifts cease with the early church? How about church, full-time ministers, and tithing? Do you reject the notion of "organized religion," believe pastors should get jobs like everyone else, and think tithing is an Old Testament principle that doesn't apply to you? What is your opinion on evangelism? Did you disagree with my thoughts on street evangelism? How about issues outside the church like education and politics? Do you believe in the value of higher education or do you think universities simply indoctrinate a younger generation? Can a Christian be a Democrat or a Republican?

If you are like me, you have an opinion concerning every one of these issues and even more on things I didn't mention. Some of these opinions are based on the things you were taught; others come through life experiences. How dead set are you on those opinions? Can you consider the possibility that your view may be slightly off at best and flat-out wrong at worst?

There is power in a made-up mind, but only if it's made up on the right things! God's truth pertains to each and every issue you and I will face in life. However, when we can only see things our way, we close our minds to His truth and become a hardheaded saint. His word can't penetrate and bear fruit in our lives because we refuse to listen. We are just like that man I met on the streets: stubborn, obstinate, and unwilling to accept truth. He couldn't receive God's truth concerning salvation. The hardheaded saint can't receive God's truth concerning their spiritual life.

For instance, a man who rejects divine healing is likely to never experience healing. You could show him every verse that pertains to healing, share testimonies of healing, pray for his healing, but if he is unreceptive to healing, it will not manifest itself in his life. There is power in a made-up mind. A made-up mind can release God's power into a situation or restrict it.

A young lady who believes that tongues and prophesy ceased with the early church and that the Pentecostal doctrine concerning the baptism of the Holy Ghost is in error will never receive the baptism. Go ahead, show her every scripture in the Old Testament and New Testament that speaks of the outpouring of the Spirit, tell her your testimony, and then lay hands on her. If she is unreceptive, she will not receive. There is power in a made-up mind. A made-up mind can receive the Holy Ghost or reject the baptism.

It is possible you've made up your mind concerning a truth that is actually causing you to forfeit its fruit. This is the dangerous power of a religious mindset. There is power in a made-up mind. A made-up mind can receive or reject the truth.

A young evangelist named Stephen came up against a mob of hardheaded religious men. As a result he became the first Christian martyr. Luke writes that Stephen was *"full of faith and power, did great wonders and signs among the people"* (Acts 6:8). There was a group of former Jewish slaves known as the Synagogue of the Freedmen who became jealous of Stephen and would come to debate him like just the Pharisees would with Jesus. However, they were *"not able to resist the wisdom and the Spirit by which he spoke"* (Acts 6:10). So they began to falsely accuse him of blasphemy in their religious court.

Stephen gives an incredible defense of his faith and then turns to his religious persecutors and calls them out, saying, *"You stiff-necked and uncircumcised in heart and ears! You always resist the Holy Spirit; as your fathers did, so do you"* (Acts 7:51). The preacher called out their hardened hearts. They were stiff-necked and hardheaded religious men who stubbornly resisted the truth concerning Christ. His words were not without effect. The Bible says that *"when they heard these things they were cut to the heart"* (Acts 7:54). However, instead of repenting and receiving the abundant life that only comes through Jesus, *"they cried out with a loud voice, stopped their ears, and ran at him with one accord; and they cast him out of the city and stoned him"* (Acts 7:57).

The truth struck their hearts. They were filled with conviction concerning what they heard preached but they didn't heed the words. Instead they stopped their ears. The truth could no longer penetrate because they were not listening. They allowed a religious mindset to solidify within them.

Not only did their religious mindsets keep them from hearing the truth, it turned them into murderers. Be assured, when you allow religious mindsets to grow in you, it starts to take away life—primarily your own.

It is interesting that these hardheaded men called themselves the Synagogue of the Freedmen. This was an ancient synagogue of liberated Jewish slaves and prisoners of war. They had once been enslaved in captivity, but now they were free. You would think that men such as these would be the last ones to be so oppressive. These were men who had been naturally set free from bondage. Now they were bound to the rules and restrictions of a religious slavery. It shows how natural it is to stiffen our necks and become hardheaded saints.

This is why we are warned to *"stand fast therefore in the liberty by which Christ has made us free, and do not be entangled again with a yoke of bondage"* (Galatians 5:1). It is easy for those who have been set free to find bondage once again. They just have to stop their ears from hearing.

Wearing the Path

Religious and rebellious mindsets don't happen overnight. They are worn into us over the years like a trail that has endured the abuse of daily foot traffic. Every day that goes by and every footprint simply hardens the heart and head that much more. We become more and more entrenched in our position and less and less receptive.

There are many feet responsible for wearing these mindsets into individuals. However, in this crowd of feet there are two that wear a path more heavily than the rest. No doubt you've felt the crushing weight of both. They are the feet of offense and tradition.

Offense is one of the quickest ways to shut off receptiveness to the things of the Spirit. Solomon wrote that *"an offended brother is more unyielding than a fortified city, and disputes are like the barred gates of a citadel"* (Proverbs 18:19). Jesus cautioned His disciples and said, *"It is impossible that no offenses should come"* (Luke 17:1). Life is going to bring many offenses your way. Most of those will come through the people who are closest to you. Be careful what you do when you're offended. Our natural tendency is to harden ourselves so that we don't get hurt again. We become a *"fortified city"* with *"barred gates."*

Jesus returned to His hometown and began to teach in the same synagogue He grew up in. At first the people marveled at His command of the truth and they wondered where He received such revelation. They had watched Him grow up. They knew His father and family. They should have celebrated Him and received Him gladly. However, *"they were offended at Him"* (Matthew 13:57). They began to belittle Him as the son of a carpenter and could not receive Him as the Son of God. Their offense caused them to become unreceptive and as such Jesus *"did not do many mighty works there because of their unbelief"* (Matthew 13:58). Their offense created an environment of unbelief and kept them from receiving from Him.

Offense is dangerous. This is why we must be quick to forgive, otherwise the offense sets in, the heart hardens, and we become unreceptive to God's word. Jesus taught that *"whenever you stand praying, if you have anything against anyone, forgive him, that your Father in heaven may also forgive you your trespasses"* (Mark 11:25). When you hold onto your hurts, your hurts take hold of you. They become barriers that keep you from receiving from the Lord.

The second foot is that of tradition. Tradition is the religious rules, rites, and rituals that are passed down from one generation to the next. Jesus said you make *"the word of God of no effect through your tradition which you have handed down"* (Mark 7:13).

The Pharisees were the epitome of tradition. These hyper-religious men were careful to observe every letter of God's law, yet missed the entire point of the law. For example, their tradition taught them to *"remember the Sabbath day to keep it holy"* (Exodus 20:8). This was a good command that taught us to observe a day of rest and focus upon the Lord. What the Pharisees missed was that *"the Sabbath was made for man, not man for the Sabbath!"* (Mark 2:27). Tradition had enslaved the religious-minded man to observe the Sabbath instead of resting in it.

Jesus was known to offend this tradition by healing people on the Sabbath. It is amusing the Pharisees considered this to be work. How dare Jesus perform a miracle on the Lord's day! Their tradition would rather leave someone blind, sick, or lame than to see them made whole on a day devoted to the Lord. It seems absurd to consider, but that's exactly what religious tradition is—absurd.

Tradition is a thief that takes the life and leaves the victim unreceptive. Jesus said that *"the thief comes to kill, steal and destroy, but I have come that you might life in all its fullness"* (John 10:10). Religious tradition has taught us to read that verse and see the devil as the thief that comes to kill, steal, and destroy.

No doubt this is exactly what Satan desires to do in your life. However, in context, Jesus is not speaking about the devil, but the religious teacher. He just finished calling them blind guides. Now He calls them thieves and hired hands who do not care for the sheep entrusted to them. Consider this paraphrase of John 10:10. The hard-headed religious man comes to kill, steal, and destroy with their traditions, which nullify the word of God and make it of no effect in your life.

This is a sentiment that Jesus drove home with a truly uplifting message found in Matthew 23 you could title, *Woe Unto You!* Here Jesus delivers eight woes directed at the hard-hearted religious teacher. He begins by calling out in a loud voice, *"Woe to you, scribes and Pharisees, hypocrites! For you shut up the kingdom of heaven against men; for you neither go in yourselves, nor do you allow those who are entering to go in. Woe to you, scribes and Pharisees, hypocrites! For you travel land and sea to win one proselyte, and when he is won, you make him twice as much a son of hell as yourselves"* (Matthew 23:14-15).

These religious teachers were guilty of wearing a path into the minds of their disciples, drilling their toxic theology, dangerous doctrine, and religious rules deep into their hearts. Jesus said you go to the extreme to capture your disciple, then leave him worse off than yourself. The eighteenth century theologian, Matthew Henry, wrote, "To unlearn that which is bad proves many times a harder task than to learn that which is good."[1] How true!

Offense and tradition are two heavy feet that wear us down over the years and build mindsets that are difficult to overcome. These strongholds inhibit our receptiveness to God's word.

Is it possible you've fallen victim to religious mindsets? Do you ever find yourself absolutely convinced you're right even when others disagree? Are you highly opinionated and love to debate? Do you receive correction and criticism well or do you become defensive? Are you quick to judge others, but easily excuse yourself? Do you have someone in authority that holds you accountable? When is the last time you found yourself repenting in prayer? Are you bitter, angry, or resentful toward someone? Are you jealous or prideful? Are you harboring unforgiveness? These questions are not meant to cause you to retreat, but to realize areas of your own life you've allowed to become fallow. A hardened heart can't hear!

Dangers of Being on the Path

The great revivalist of the Second Great Awakening, Charles Finney, spoke of the dangers of finding yourself on the wayside. He said, "It will do no good to preach to you while your hearts are in this hardened, and waste, and fallow state. The farmer might just as well sow his grain on the rock. It will bring forth no fruit. This is the reason why there are so many fruitless ministers in the Church, and why there is so much organization and so little deep-toned feeling."[2]

This is a precarious place to be because the religious or rebellious mindset creates an environment that is unreceptive to truth. Remember, Paul wrote, *"How, then, can they call on the one they have not believed in? And how can they believe in the one of whom they have not heard? And how can they hear without someone preaching to them?"* Paul continues, *"Consequently, faith comes from hearing the message, and the message is heard through the word about Christ"* (Romans 10:14,17).

Faith comes by hearing! If I cannot hear, or refuse to hear, I will not have faith. This is the inherent danger of fallowed ground. It creates a faithless environment that will not produce any spiritual fruit. If you can't hear then you will not have faith.

Jesus said it like this: *"And you shall know the truth, and the truth shall make you free"* (John 8:32). If you know the truth, you will know true freedom. However, if I hear no truth, I will have no freedom. Your faith and freedom in the Spirit is directly tied to your ability to hear. So many find themselves without faith and without freedom because they refuse to hear. They've allowed the offenses and traditions to create religious and rebellious mindsets that have shut their ears. Like an immature child, their fingers are in their ears as they sing, "I can't hear you! I'm not listening! La-la, la-la, la lah!"

BREAKING UP THE FALLOWED GROUND

My friend if you find fallow ground within your heart it's time to take up the plow and let the soil be turned over. The process can be painful, but it is necessary to cultivate a truly receptive spirit to the voice of God.

The only way to till up the hardened path that keeps you on the wayside is to fall upon your knees and repent. Repentance is a beautiful word and an incredible work of God's grace. Invite the Holy Spirit to come and turn over the soil of your life. Let Him reveal the places where you have made up your mind on the wrong things. Let Him show you the places where your soil is unreceptive and therefore infertile to God's truth.

Pray as David prayed: *"Search me, O God, and know my heart; try me, and know my anxieties; and see if there is any wicked way in me, and lead me in the way everlasting"* (Psalm 139:23-24).

Allow the Lord to show you the sin in your life you've overlooked. The ingratitude, the lack of love, the neglect of His word and time in prayer. Let Him reveal your unbelief and your secret motivations. Let Him convict you concerning the lost and your silent voice. Let Him stir you to holiness, humility, and self-denial. I know these are not the sins we often concentrate on. We focus on what we consider to be the big sins and take great pride when they no longer mark our lives. However these sins are just as detrimental to our faith. Left unchecked, they harden the soil.

The path to receptivity begins with a plow. If the Lord is speaking to you, don't resist. Let the fallowed ground within your heart be loosened. You can trust that Jesus knows how to cut us deep enough to break us open, but not so deep as to break us.

> *Holy Spirit, search me and reveal my heart. Show me the hardened places I've allowed to grow fallow. I want to see truth. I understand that I am unaware of all the places I have allowed religious opinions of man and false assumptions to cloud my view. Show me the secret sins that keep me from hearing truth.*

NOTES

1. Matthew Henry, *Matthew Henry's Commentary on the Whole Bible* (Hendrickson Publishers, 1994), 2096.
2. Charles G. Finney, *Lectures on Revivals of Religion* (Boston, MA: John P Jewett & Co, 1858). 43.

Chapter Four

Thou Shalt Be Tested

The trials and tests of your faith

"Those on the rock are the ones who receive the word with joy when they hear it, but they have no root. They believe for a while, but in the time of testing they fall away."
—LUKE 8:13, NIV

RINGING OUT

There is a tradition that exists amongst the US Navy SEAL that offers a fascinating analogy in regards to our faith. It's the dividing line between those who rise to a greater faith and those who fall from it. It's why so few accomplish great things for the kingdom, while so many do so little. It's known as "ringing the bell."

Ringing the bell is the exit door for a hopeful SEAL cadet who realizes they cannot make it through what is unquestionably the toughest training in the world. Can't take the pain and punishment anymore? Just go ring the bell and it will all be over. Ready to give in to what your flesh is screaming at you to do? Go ahead, drop out. Don't have what it takes? There is a bell with your name on it.

Spiritually speaking, our nation is filled with multitudes who have rung out of the faith. As they faced their own trials and tests they opted to bail out. Cultivating a receptive spirit means making up your mind now that no bell will be ringing in your future. Every obstacle you face is a disguised opportunity for divine possibility. You have to choose to see the adversity as a chance for growth. Trials and tests of various kinds are going to come—the question is, will you let them discipline you or destroy you? That answer is entirely up to you.

Our Navy SEALs are among the most elite soldiers in the world. They are the best of the best. It's this notoriety that inspires hundreds of men to attempt to join the ranks of this special force each year. However, only 20 percent of those who seek to become a SEAL actually have what it takes to persevere through the nine months of grueling training required.

That sobering reality is established from the very first day of SEAL training. Each candidate is instructed to look around the room at the person to their right, left, front, and back. They are then informed that only one of those individuals will still be there at the end of training. The rest will be ringing the bell. The instructor knows it is his job to put the class to the test and find that one out of the five that has what it takes to truly be a SEAL.

It would surprise you at who makes it. Like a school-yard pick you'd likely single out the biggest, most athletic guys to be your best bet to emerge from the crowd. Many times these are some of the first out. Becoming a SEAL is not about who can do the most push-ups, run the fastest, or lift the most weight. It's about who can persevere. Who has what it takes to handle the mental stress of being constantly yelled at, ripped apart, and put down, while at the same time being put through physically punishing environments.[1]

The trainee's day begins early each morning on what is appropriately named the Grinder. This is a slab of concrete and asphalt that sits in the center of the training facility. The Grinder is where most of their physical training initiates. Each day, as the group assembles on the Grinder, less and less are present.

That dreaded brass bell is suspended from a pole off to the side of the Grinder. Its presence is always felt. An ever-growing collection of green helmets lines the ground beneath the bell, each with the number and name of a recruit who couldn't make it through the training. Everyone knows they have the option to quit at any time. All they have to do is go ring the bell three times, and leave their helmet behind with all the others.

When a cadet decides to drop out, they are given the opportunity to change their mind. The instructor challenges them before they ring the bell, encouraging them to go back. Some do, but every instructor knows that once a cadet has approached the bell once, it's only a matter of time before he will be back ringing out. The reason is simple: once quitting becomes an option, eventually you will.[2]

Weeding out the quitters and finding those rare few who never let the idea of quitting enter into their mind is the purpose of the rigorous training. The instructors are looking for the best. They push the cadet's body and mind beyond what they previously thought was possible. They break them down to see who refuses to break.

Nothing demonstrates this more than the notorious Hell Week. This is the most brutal part of the training and is as much a test of the cadet's character as it is training. The Navy describes this week as "a test of physical endurance, mental tenacity and true teamwork where 2/3 or more of your class may call it quits or "ring the bell." Physical discomfort and pain will cause many to decide it isn't worth it. The miserable wet-cold approaching hypothermia will make others quit. Sheer fatigue and sleep deprivation will cause every candidate to question his core values, motivations, limits, and everything he's made of and stands for."[3]

You may wonder what the secret is to enduring such excruciating training and the key to emerging victorious in the end. I believe it is best summed up by former Navy Seal Ron Seiple, a combat-decorated veteran who served two tours in Vietnam. He said, "You don't ever let quitting enter your mind as it is a sickness that will weaken you."[4]

Sounds a lot like something Paul wrote: *"But put on the Lord Jesus Christ, and make no provision for the flesh, to fulfill its lusts"* (Romans 13:4). Make no allowance for the flesh! Don't give doubt, lust, fear, or pride a foothold within your life. If you do, it's a sickness that will weaken you and eventually take you out.

I am thankful for the men and women of our armed forces who so courageously give of themselves for the sake of our freedom. There is so much we can glean and learn from these heroes. So much of their training and tactics are applicable to our spiritual lives. That is why military themes and analogies play such an important role in scripture. What these soldiers demonstrate in the natural world can teach us much about the supernatural battle we all face.

Jesus didn't come to earth to raise up a church filled with lazy, lethargic laity, but to raise up a bold battalion of believers. Quitting is not a concept that should ever enter into the mind of a believer. Saying "yes" to following Christ is not a temporary commitment, it is an eternal one. There is no expiration date on this covenant. This is why Christ cautioned His would-be disciples to count the cost before taking up their cross. He said it would be far better for them to never begin than to make it half way and then drop out when things get tough (Luke 14:25-33).

This sets the context for the next soil mentioned by Jesus: *"Those on the rock are the ones who receive the word with joy when they hear it, but they have no root. They believe for a while, but in the time of testing they fall away"* (Luke 8:13, NIV).

We have already discussed how a hardened heart creates an unreceptive spirit to the word of God. Likewise, a heart that lacks depth is also unreceptive. However, unlike the hardened path that never shows any signs of life, this shallow soil deceptively shows the initial sprouts of life. These individuals gladly hear and receive the word. The word plants itself within their hearts and begins to grow, but because it has no root it doesn't take long before the new life quickly dries up *"in the time of testing."*

No one should be naive. Jesus made it clear that times of testing would come our way. There are seasons when life and the enemy will be allowed to test your faith. When those times come will you remain steadfast or will the shallowness of your faith be revealed?

Each and every day you step out onto your own Grinder and what you believe is put to the test. Some days the sun shines, the temperature is pleasant, and those with shallow faith remain unaware of their own lack of depth in their faith. Then storms start to come, or the heat of the sun starts to bare down. Is quitting an option in those moments?

Remember, the moment you allow quitting to become an option, eventually you will. As Jesus said these people in the time of testing *"fall away."*

FALLEN BELIEVERS

We have seen far too many fallen believers. They were moved with emotion during a message—maybe they were at a low in their life and saw the hope offered in Christ as their way out. However, when the emotions changed, their belief did as well. They needed Jesus for the moment, or signed up without counting the full cost. When the first trial or test came their way they rung out.

Contemporary Christianity has fostered an easy believe-ism. We have shared the benefits of becoming a believer, but have not spoken of the cost to truly follow Christ. Jesus was quick to tell those would-be disciples that following Him meant picking up a cross of their own. Today ministers have created a cross without cost. We celebrate the price Christ paid, but speak nothing of the price we pay. Jesus gave His all for us—we in turn must give our all for Him.

Today we invite sinners to receive Christ by praying a simple prayer. We write their name on a piece of paper, add them to our salvation scorecard, and then send them on their merry way. We fail to tell them that salvation means death to self. We don't inform them of the trials and tests that are sure to come their way if they truly meant what they prayed.

Everyone enjoys the idea of Heaven and eternal life. No one wants to spend eternity in the fires of Hell. However deciding to walk the straight and narrow path of Christianity may mean enduring the onslaught of Hell as you walk here on earth. Jesus didn't promise to spare us from the storms of life, but He did promise to walk with us through those storms.

Today studies reveal that 83 percent of our nation professes belief in Jesus and considers themselves to be Christian.[5] But do they have true belief? Let a time of tribulation and persecution strike the Church and we will quickly see how many shallow believers clear out. When their faith is put to the test will their behavior bear out their belief, or reveal them to be simply pretenders?

These are the ones Jesus was referring to in the parable. They received the word gladly, but because they had no roots they fall away when the tests come. They embody the verse that states, *"These people draw near to Me with their mouth, and honor Me with their lips, but their heart is far from Me"* (Matthew 15:8).

Where is this message being preached today? We tell people come to Jesus and you will be blessed and find prosperity. While it is true that blessings and prosperity is God's reward for those who diligently seek Him, don't be so carnally minded to believe that blessings must always be measured in silver and gold.

Not too long ago, a young Christian named Yasmine reached out to me from Pakistan. She was doubting her faith and wanted prayer. I spent several weeks encouraging her. Then all was silent. I wasn't sure if she had walked away or if she was continuing to grow. Then I received an email from her. She was in a hospital.

With an emboldened faith, she went to a remote village in Pakistan to share the Gospel. She wrote with great excitement of the fact that over one hundred people were saved as she preached with authority, many of which were Muslim. However, as she was leaving, she and her friends were attacked by several men in the village. The men threatened them with guns, beat the team, and stole all their belongings including their Bibles. She wrote, "I am injured so badly. More than my other team members because I was the one who preached the Gospel. They warned me not to come here again otherwise they would kill me."

I wrote Yasmine back and told her that she was a hero. Here in the midst of her pain she was rejoicing that one hundred lost men and women came to know Jesus. Yasmine asked that I keep her in my prayers so that she could continue to "go preach the Gospel."

A few weeks earlier she doubted God and her faith. Now she is celebrating from a hospital at the salvation of souls. My friend, this woman of God understood something most Western Christians never will about the true blessings and benefits of kingdom prosperity. Jesus said, *"Blessed are you when they persecute you for my name's sake for great is your reward in heaven"* (Matthew 5:11-12). Yasmine can tell you about that blessing!

Today churches call people to a much different Christianity than Christ Himself called people to. We say, "Come to Jesus, He will make everything OK." He said, *"Come to me and bring along a cross"* (Luke 9:23). We say, "Come to Jesus and you'll find prosperity." He said, *"Come to me and you'll find persecution"* (John 15:20). We say, "Come to Jesus and you'll live." He said, *"Come to me and die"* (Luke 9:24). For the Christian, dying is the best way to live!

It is no wonder why we have so many religious professors of Christ, but so few radical believers in Christ! My friend, you will be tested. Your faith will be tried by the fires of life and only that which is pure will remain. Make no allowance for the flesh! There is no room to quit. No bell should be ringing in your future.

SHALLOW BELIEVERS

As I have stated before, the parable wasn't just given to the multitudes—it was also directed at the disciples. We must not make the mistake of opting for the simplistic meaning that this shallow, rocky soil can only be the individual who falls away from saving faith. It also applies to the areas of our own life where we don't allow the truth of God's word to fully penetrate deep in us. This is where the religious crowd and religious mentalities truly live. Their faith is all in their head, but the moment it is required to manifest in real life, they ring out.

Many choose to sit comfortably in the cushy chairs of cozy little churches, refusing to step out into the world where faith is truly manifest. They can give you their doctrines, theology, and fundamental truths. They have their theories and can talk for hours about the things of the Spirit, but it is all in their heads. Their problem is the truth has never left the place of intellect and found its way into their heart where it has anchored itself as a core belief. If you have to think about something, it's not in your heart yet. The head thinks; the heart speaks.

The shallow believer lives here. They know the facts, the stories, and even memorize scripture. They mistakenly equate this with belief. It's not what you know in your head that will save you, it's what you believe in your heart! There is a difference between knowing something and believing something. One is a matter of the head, the other the heart.

This is where the trials and tests of our faith come into play. James writes, "*Consider it pure joy, my brothers and sisters, whenever you face trials of many kinds, because you know that the testing of your faith produces perseverance. Let perseverance finish its work so that you may be mature and complete, not lacking anything*" (James 1:2-4 NIV).

The Bible says to consider it *pure joy* when you face the trials and tests of life. We are challenged to do the exact opposite of what comes natural. Instead of dropping your head in defeat, James says to throw a party in the face of your adversity. Where most would moan and groan about their test, we are encouraged to celebrate.

Picture this: you go out to the mailbox and find an unexpected bill. You know there is not enough in your bank account to cover the expense—your upcoming paycheck is already budgeted. You haven't mismanaged your finances or lived beyond your means. You've freely given to the Lord. Now, your heart starts to sink, as you hear the thunder of this approaching financial storm. Your natural reaction should be to lower your head in defeat, but instead joy springs up from the inside. You begin to dance and shout beside your mailbox.

Your neighbor steps out of their house assuming you just won the lottery. They ask what the celebration is all about. You respond, "I just got a bill I can't pay!"

"Wait a minute? Why are you celebrating, then?"

"Because I'm being tested! My God is about to come through for me in a way that will surprise those who hear about it and it will build a greater faith within me and the faith of others around me!"

Imagine you are sitting across the desk from a doctor who has just returned with the results of a test. His face is solemn; he begins to tell you that the diagnosis is not good. He is recommending immediate treatment and offers little hope. Your natural reaction should be to fall apart as you now stare death in the face, but unspeakable joy begins to flow from the fountain of your spirit. You stand up and start to dance and praise the Lord.

The doctor looks at you confused. He says, "I don't think you understand. This is bad news."

You say, "I don't think you understand. I'm celebrating in the face of my trial. God is about to come through for me in a way that will give glory to Him and strengthen my faith."

Trials and tests are a part of life. As certain as the sun will rise tomorrow, you can anticipate another test. Rather than dread them, embrace them! They are opportunities for us to measure what we know, to learn what we don't and to grow through the process. The trials and tests increase our receptiveness.

This is why we should consider each test as an opportunity for great joy. When your faith is tested, your faith is increased. A weightlifter understands that true growth is painful. The physical pain he feels burning in his muscles is an indication of growth. He learns to take pleasure in his pain because he knows that the pain is producing strength. Likewise we can take pleasure in our painful tests because we know that they are producing strength within us. The pain is temporary but the outcome is not. The test develops the strength of endurance and makes us perfect, complete, and in need of nothing.

Jesus often placed His disciples in the midst of a situation that He knew would test their faith. One of these tests takes place upon the Sea of Galilee. *"Jesus got into the boat and started across the lake with His disciples. Suddenly, a fierce storm struck the lake, with waves breaking into the boat. Jesus was sleeping. The disciples went and woke Him up, shouting, 'Lord, save us! We're going to drown!' Jesus responded, 'Why are you afraid? You have so little faith!' Then He got up and rebuked the wind and waves, and suddenly there was a great calm. The disciples were amazed. 'Who is this man?' they asked. 'Even the winds and waves obey him'*" (Matthew 8:23-27 NLT).

Notice the stark contrast between Jesus and the disciples as they face this storm. Jesus, full of faith, is at rest in the midst of a storm that has everyone else fearful for their lives. What a blessed place to find. A person can be in the valley of the shadow of death, yet be at perfect peace. Jesus is the quintessential example of what true faith looks like and reveals the faith available to us.

The disciples give us an example of what *so little faith* or shallow faith looks like in the midst of a trial or test. It would be reasonable to assume that when the disciples first got in the boat hours earlier they did so without any hesitance or fear. They would have set out upon the waters in confidence. This was their trade—they were experts at sailing this lake. They were at peace as long as the waters were peaceful. When the external conditions around them changed, they did as well. Their faith was dependent on circumstances. Jesus's wasn't. His faith came from within and was independent of the circumstances. This test revealed the faith of both Jesus and the disciples.

I wonder how the shallow-faith religious believers might have instructed the disciples as they faced the storm. You know who I'm taking about. These are the ones who have their theories and theologies at the ready just waiting to enlighten you with their truth as you face your test. They circle around the afflicted like vultures offering simplistic spiritual-sounding solutions that work well in a sermon but fail in the storm.

One preacher might shout at Peter to lay hands on the boat and begin to confess things that are not as though they are. "Peter, lay hands on that boat! Confess that it's a luxury yacht not a meager little fishing boat. Command prosperity to come to you out on the waves in the midst of your storm. Can't you feel the breeze? The wind is blowing prosperity your way!"

Another preacher pulls out his guitar and encourages John and the disciples to go ahead and praise God in the midst of this storm. "Praise your way through the pouring rain! Worship those waves away! Come sing with me, 'The Lord told Noah to build him an arkie, arkie.'" Don't like that one? How about, "Let it rain, let it rain! Open the flood gates of Heaven, let it rain, let it rain!" No? Want something more contemporary? "I want to go deeper, but I don't know how to swim."

Then the next preacher comes along touting the power of positive confessions. He says, "God wants you to change your mind concerning this storm. He has freed us from the curse of the storm. You're the head not the tail! Go ahead, confess this with me. There is no storm! There is no lightning! There are no waves! Don't confess the storm, Thomas! Deny it! That storm doesn't exist. The waves are just your doubts trying to manifest."

The final preacher brings a big Bible to the storm and says, "You need to start quoting scripture at it. Here, take this King James Bible, hold it up in front of the storm, and read Psalm 23: '*Yea, though I walk through the valley of the shadow of death, I will fear no evil: for thou art with me.*' Read Psalm 91: '*A thousand shall fall at thy side, and ten thousand at thy right hand; but it shall not come nigh thee.*'"

Please don't get me wrong, I believe there is truth in standing in faith, confessing God's word, and praising God in the midst of your storm. I am not making light of Bbib-lical truth. When these things come from a sincere faith they are powerful. I am pointing out man's tendency to create theological routines out of our extremes. I've found that the cute Christian clichés offered up in a sermon might get shouted down on a Sunday but often fall apart come Monday. When I am facing a storm, I don't need the dogmatic doctrine of man's persuasion—I want a divine demonstration of God's power!

This is the purpose of the storm and the reason for the test. It puts to the fire the things we think we know and reveals what we truly believe. The test separates that which is and is not of faith. The test uncovers the rocky places within our hearts and heads. It exposes the mindsets and mentalities that are restricting our receptivity. If we let the test accomplish its work within us these rocks are rooted out and our faith is built up.

James says, "*Consider it pure joy, my brothers and sisters, whenever you face trials of many kinds.*" Not only is there a test guaranteed in your future, James says you will find yourself encompassed in the midst of *many kinds* of trials. There is a wide variety of tests you are likely to face. Each has a different function in the strengthening of your faith. I'll give you a few examples of tests you are likely to face.

Temptations

These are the thoughts and impulses that pull on your flesh to do something contrary to the nature of God. Temptations come internally from our own desires and externally from others. Temptation is something we all experience. It is important to note that temptation is not sin, but giving into temptation is.

James tells us that we are tempted by our own desires. You will only be tempted by something that already has a place within your heart. Pay attention to what grabs your attention.

Our attractions reveal the intentions of the heart! The temptations you face have much to say about the rocky places that reside within your heart.

Temptations show us the parts of ourselves that are still tied to the old sinful flesh. These are areas that have yet to be fully surrendered to the Lord. When you are tempted, stop and ask yourself, "Why is this a temptation for me?" Then take it to the Lord in prayer. Be honest and transparent before Him. He has promised that He will "*not allow the temptation to be more than you can stand. When you are tempted, He will show you a way out so that you can endure*" (1 Corinthians 10:13).

Hardships

These are adverse situations and circumstances that are brought on by life. Sometimes they are the consequence of our own decisions. Other times they are brought on by the decisions of others. Understand that everything is Father filtered. God sees the storm coming our way and decides for our own good and for His glory to allow us to enter the storm. He doesn't do it to tear us down, but to build us up.

A disciplined disciple is the Lord's intention. Self-discipline is the fruit of a Spirit-filled life. Discipline is not the ability to do the right thing once, but the ability to consistently do the right thing every time. God disciplines us in love so that we will become disciplined.

Not all discipline comes in the way of punishment. That is a very negative view of discipline. Choose to embrace discipline as a positive thing. Yes, there are times it is corrective. This too is a positive thing. God isn't looking to hurt you—He wants to help you. It is because He loves us that He corrects us to teach us His ways. Other times His discipline comes to sharpen us. The Lord will target an area of our life to increase our strength in that area because He sees the necessity of it in our future.

When you are facing hardship, ask yourself, "What is it I am supposed to be learning?" Journal your thoughts and prayers during these times. Take note of what God is speaking to you. What brought this trial my way? Is this the product of my own choosing? If so, what do I need to correct? Is it the product of someone else's doing? How do I need to respond?

No one gets to exempt a test from the Lord. If you fail to learn the lesson needed in this present trial, you are likely to see the same test again until you pass it. Learning to humbly yield to the trials and tests of the Lord is the fastest way to expedite your learning process.

Choices

Every day you are faced with a whole host of decisions. Some are of little consequence while others carry great significance. Our decisions determine our destiny. There are times you will be faced with a moral decision. Will you choose to do what is right regardless the outcome? Other times you are faced with a pivotal decision. These decisions can alter our careers, locations, and direction. They should not be taken lightly. Other times you face leaps of faith. You feel the prompting of the still-small voice to step out and do the impossible. Will you obey or resist?

Choice is the greatest gift God gave mankind. No one serves God by coercion. We choose to serve Him. Since your decisions chart your direction, make sure you choose wisely. Thankfully, when life presents you with a choice, God doesn't remain silent. He offers His wisdom and makes it freely available to those who know how to listen.

Persecution

Jesus warned that persecution would come upon those who followed Him. Standing up for Christ or what is right will not always be popular. There are times when your faith will cost you friends, self-esteem, careers, and in some cases your life. Those who are afraid of ridicule will fail this test every time while those who have fully surrendered their life to Christ will find their faith emboldened. When we are persecuted for the sake of Christ we become part of a rare brotherhood. The Bible calls it "*the fellowship of Christ's sufferings*" (Philippians 3:10). The benefits of this fellowship is a greater level of intimacy with the Lord. It is a secret place that is reserved for those who have truly counted the cost and followed Him.

Purpose of the Test

> "*Dear friends, don't be surprised at the fiery trials you are going through, as if something strange were happening to you. Instead, be very glad—for these trials make you partners with Christ in his suffering, so that you will have the wonderful joy of seeing his glory when it is revealed to all the world*" (1 Peter 4:12-13).

The trials and tests of our faith should not catch us by surprise. When they come we can take joy in them because we know there is a purpose. James says, "*Know that the testing of your faith produces perseverance. Let perseverance finish its work so that you may be mature and complete, not lacking anything*" (James 1:3-4).

A farmer reaps his harvest during the heat of the day. You may be facing the fiery heat of a trial or test, but don't let your present position pull your eyes off the future fruit. There is a reward for passing through this fire. Maturity is the purpose of the test.

God places us upon the Grinder not so that He can see what we are made of, but so that we can see what we are made of. The test has an uncanny ability to introduce you to yourself. It is impossible to know what you really believe unless you are tested.

When a man is tempted by lust and he chooses to give in to that temptation what does that say about the man? It reveals that lust already in his heart. It shows him that what he is relying on is wrong. If he heeds the lesson in the test, repents, confesses his faults, and learns to lean on the Lord, he grows in maturity. His ability to persevere in the face of temptation will increase. The next time the temptation comes along, he sees it for what it is and chooses to remove the source of temptation. He is growing in wisdom.

A mature faith is the ultimate aim of the trials and tests. The test itself is an excellent teacher that helps us grow. So, let it *grow*! Remember there is gain in the pain! If there is a test, then there is a reason. If there is a reason, then there is a reward. Persevere through the fire, for when your endurance is fully developed, you will be perfect and complete, needing nothing.

Finally, let me point out the most important aspect of any trial or test you face. As you face your storm, know that you are not alone! Though you may feel that you are by yourself, that is not the case. As the disciples fretted over their storm and started to fear that their death was eminent someone took notice of the fact that Jesus was in the boat with them. There, Jesus was at perfect peace, resting in the same storm that threatened them.

There is a similar place of rest in the midst of your test. As the storm rages all around you, there is a place you can quiet yourself and find the peace of His presence. The disciples should have let the peace they saw on Jesus's face instill peace within them. Instead they called to Him in fear rather than faith. The shallowness of their faith was revealed. They didn't pass this test. Likewise you will not pass every test you face. Keep going. Learn from your mistakes. Even though the disciples called out to Jesus in fear, Jesus still came to their rescue. He silenced the storm. The disciples witnessed Jesus command the wind and waves with His words. They marveled at what kind of man could do such things. What an amazing revelation they had of Him in the midst of their storm!

In the midst of your test you can call out to Him in faith and see Him manifest His power as well. It's hard to ride through the storm, but it will subside. When it finally clears you'll discover the opportunity.

We have an expression that we like to use with our leaders. We tell them, "Way to grow!" It's our recognition that every accomplishment they make is a testament to their own spiritual growth. They are maturing before our eyes as they endure their own personal trials and tests. Instead of saying "way to go"—which acknowledges solely what they can do—we say "way to grow" as an acknowledgment of what God is doing in them. They are allowing Him to cultivate the soil of their lives, removing the rocky places and becoming more and more receptive.

May I also say to you, "Way to grow!" Keep persevering through the trials and tests. Despise the sound of the bell, make no allowance for it in your Christian walk. Let the test accomplish its full purpose in your life.

Thank You Lord for the trials and tests of my faith. I know You are at work in the shallow places within me to increase my faith and my receptiveness to Your word. You are with me in this storm—help me learn and grow through this season.

NOTES

1. Webb, Brandon; Mann, John David, *The Red Circle: My Life in the Navy SEAL Sniper Corps and How I Trained America's Deadliest Marksmen* (St. Martin's Press, 2012). 93
2. Marcus Luttrell, *Lone Survivor: The Eyewitness Account of Operation Redwing and the Lost Heroes of SEAL Team 10* (New York, NY: Little, Brown and Company, 2007), 136.
3. NavySEALS.com, "BUD/S (Basic Underwater Demolition/SEAL) Training," http://navyseals.com/nsw/bud-s-basic-underwater-demolition-seal-training/.
4. Todd Kuslikis, "24 Elite Navy SEALs Reveal the Secret to Their Toughness and How They Made It Through Hell Week," A Shot of Adrenaline, http://ashotofadrenaline.net/navy-seals-how-they-made-it-through-hell-week/.
5. Gary Langer, "Poll: Most Americans Say They're Christian," ABC News, http://abcnews.go.com/US/story?id=90356.

Chapter Five

The Danger of Duplicity

How being double-minded deactivates your faith

"The seed that fell among thorns stands for those who hear, but as they go on their way they are choked by life's worries, riches and pleasures, and they do not mature."
—Luke 8:14, NIV

"Ladies and gentlemen, we are having a problem with the plane and will be making an emergency landing." Those are not words you want to hear when you're flying. You can imagine the fear that announcement would ignite.

I was on a short flight from Dallas to Tulsa for a weekend of ministry. Our expectations were high as we felt that the Lord was preparing to move powerfully during the services. The flight was not full, and I was able to upgrade to first class for free. This was my first time to fly first class and though the flight was brief, being in the front of the aircraft was a blessing. It seemed that the Lord was already kissing the trip from the very beginning.

As we approached the airport to land the captain's voice broke through the peaceful silence to inform us that there was a problem. He shared that the situation was fairly routine but we would be forced to make an emergency landing. I've flown a lot and I know that there is nothing routine about an emergency landing. I trusted his words that there was little reason for alarm, but that didn't stop me from feeling somewhat fearful. This is a natural reaction when we find ourselves facing uncertain situations.

The pilot continued to reassure the passengers that he expected no issues—however, his next statement didn't help ease any fears. He said that as a precaution we would be greeted on the runway with several emergency vehicles including a "crash car." Now, at ten thousand feet in the air traveling over three hundred miles per hour the word *crash* is not something you want to hear.

I thought to myself, "Great! My first and last time I'll ever fly first class!" Deep within my spirit I knew everything would be all right. Still there was nothing I could do to stop the emotion of fear that was presently battling for control of my thoughts. All I could do was pray. I trusted if the Lord brought us to this city it wasn't to make a connection to Heaven.

As we approached the runway you could feel the anxiousness of those on board the plane. You could hear the whispers of prayers being spoken underneath everyone's breath. The plane hit the ground hard and fast. It was scary, but we were safe. Our captain did a fantastic job of landing the plane without incident. We waved in relief at the emergency vehicles that were waiting on us as we passed them by. As for the weekend in Tulsa, it was powerful! Hundreds responded to the Lord in the altars of the church.

It is amazing how quickly fear can enter into our minds even when we are in the midst of a faith-filled environment. Everything can be going great, then suddenly the unexpected takes place and fear enters the picture battling for dominion over your mind.

I am a man of faith and I strive every day to walk in a greater level of faith. I have learned that the fact that fear is present doesn't diminish faith—it actually provides an opportunity to increase faith. The key is understanding that though I may experience the emotion of fear, I do not have to live in an environment of fear. You don't get to choose your emotions, but you can choose your environment. You make the decision where those emotions will take you. Will fear drive you to a greater place of faith in the Lord, or will fear become your permanent home?

We discussed how the trials and tests of our faith are necessary to bring maturity to the shallow depths of our faith. James encourages us to celebrate our trials while understanding they are working to make our faith stronger. He continues with this thought: *"Ask in faith, with no doubting, for he who doubts is like a wave of the sea driven and tossed by the wind. For let not that man suppose that he will receive anything from the Lord; he is a double-minded man, unstable in all his ways"* (James 1:6-8).

Doubt is crippling to faith—it is the consequence of fear that has been left unchallenged. When the mind is overcome with doubt our direction becomes determined from outside forces rather than faith. James calls that being double-minded and shares that such a person receives nothing from the Lord. Doubt deactivates faith.

Have you ever asked why your faith isn't working? Why is it that someone remains unhealed when the word gives us full assurance of our healing? Why are people not walking in the promises and blessings of God that guarantee provisions within His word? Why are people not experiencing the abundant life Jesus promised filled with joy unspeakable?

I ask these type questions a lot and have found an answer within the parable of the sower. Jesus said, "*The seed that fell among thorns stands for those who hear, but as they go on their way they are choked by life's worries, riches and pleasures, and they do not mature*" (Luke 8:14). The truth of His word is choked out by the cares of this world. Earthly matters grow like weeds and hinder our receptivity. We become indecisive and full of doubt. As James says, "*for let not that man suppose that he will receive anything from the Lord*" (James 1:7).

Is it possible there are present thorns restricting and stunting your growth? There may be more than you realize. Whether it is a simple decision like choosing a restaurant or picking a new outfit to more significant decisions like starting a business, who to marry, or striving to faithfully obey the still-small voice of the Lord, it is human nature to doubt. When the situation is light those doubts are of little consequence, but when it comes to more pressing matters our doubt is dangerous. Doubt causes us to become double-minded and unsure of ourselves and decisions. Being double-minded is dangerous because it deactivates faith!

This is the picture of the individual Jesus paints as He continues to explain the parable of the soils. He now comes to the third type of soil that fails to produce a harvest. This one He compares to a field that is filled with thorns. He explains that the thorns represent the worries, riches, and pleasures of this life and shares that these things restrict His word, causing the hearer to remain "immature."

Immaturity is a great word for the condition many believers occupy and the reason so few bear any genuine fruit. It is why people pray prayers that never get answered. It's why Christians remain content with the lesser gifts of the Spirit instead of contending for the greater gifts.

These believers have read the word and even memorized many of their favorite scriptures. They've faithfully attended their churches and would be considered outstanding members of their congregations. They know the word, believe it, and have planted it into their heart. However, at the same time they allow that seed of the word to be challenged by seeds of doubt and fear. Because of this the seed that should bear fruit will never mature to produce an abundance of fruit in their lives.

Make this personal. You know what the word says about the current situation you are facing. You know what you believe. However, that does not stop fear from coming to weaken your faith. The fear grips your emotions and questions of doubt begin to flood your mind. If left unchecked these things start to settle within your heart. Now you are double-minded and your faith is deactivated.

The danger of being double-minded cannot be stressed enough. Jesus marveled at His doubting disciples and chastised them for letting their doubts get the best of them. On one occasion Jesus comes upon nine of His disciples who have been trying unsuccessfully to bring deliverance to a demon-possessed boy. A desperate father brought his son to the disciples in the hopes of saving his life. He said that his son was suicidal, often throwing himself into water or fire. I imagine the disciples laid hands on the child and prayed for some time. They bound and loosed. They laid hands and shouted. They tried everything they knew. However, as time passed it became obvious to the father and the crowd that the disciples were being defeated by this devil.

When Jesus arrives, there is a great deal of commotion. The multitudes and the scribes are arguing with the disciples. The disciples are embarrassed as they are mocked for their inability to drive out the demon. They found themselves in the midst of a situation many fear. What if I publicly pray for someone and they are not healed?

When I was a young man, fresh in my faith, I encountered a demon-possessed man at a fast-food restaurant. I was there with a group of friends. We had all noticed the eccentric man walking around the restaurant disturbing the patrons. It seemed everyone was bothered with the man, but no one was willing to do anything about him. I approached him—he asked for some money; I gave him a few bills and told him that Jesus loved him and had a plan for his life. The conversation didn't go much further.

Later he approached the table we were sitting at and began to harass one of the young ladies at our table. I stood up, placed my hand on his shoulder, and said, "In Jesus's name, I am telling you to leave!"

I'd like to tell you the man was delivered and revival broke out in the middle of the restaurant, but that's not what happened. He began to shout and yell at the top of his lungs, "You've been oppressing me for years!"

Now every eye in the restaurant was on the two of us. Here I was with my hand on a man who sounded like he was in fear for his life. I freaked out. Almost immediately the police arrived at the location, as the manager had dialed 911 earlier. They came in and escorted the man to the back of a squad car.

I was embarrassed and felt like a failure at that moment. This was my first encounter with a demon-possessed man and

I wondered why I stood paralyzed in fear rather than boldly casting that devil out.

I imagine this is what the disciples were feeling. Embarrassed that this deliverance escaped them, now they were the ridicule of the multitudes. When Jesus arrives and learns what has happened He admonishes them: *"O faithless generation, how long shall I be with you? How long shall I bear with you?"* (Mark 9:19).

Jesus called out their immature faith and unbelief in front of the crowd. As embarrassing as the ridicule of the crowd was, it couldn't compare to the sting of this rebuke. No one likes to be disciplined, especially in public. Thankfully, Jesus doesn't mind humiliating us when necessary in order to produce humility within us. As believers we have two options: be humbled or be humiliated. A temporary strike to our prideful ego is a small price to pay if it produces lasting Christlike humility within us.

The father of the boy pleads with Jesus: *"If you can do anything, have compassion on us and help us"* (Mark 9:22). Jesus responds with a powerful statement. He says, *"If you can believe, all things are possible to him who believes"* (Mark 9:23). Then Jesus does with a few words what the disciples could not do with many words. He casts the devil out and the boy is immediately set free.

Once again the disciples wait until they are alone with Jesus and come to Him privately to ask why they had failed. They wanted to know why their faith didn't work in this situation. Jesus told them, *"Because of your unbelief; for assuredly, I say to you, if you have faith as a mustard seed, you will say to this mountain, 'Move from here to there,' and it will move; and nothing will be impossible for you. However, this kind does not go out except by prayer and fasting"* (Matthew 17:20-21).

Their unbelief? Surely the disciples believed! They had seen healing and deliverance with their own eyes. Jesus had sent them out two by two and had given them authority to cast out devils. They came back to Him testifying of the healing and deliverance they had worked in His name. They saw nothing different about this time. They did it the same way they had done it in the past, yet this time it didn't work. What were they doing wrong?

That is human nature. We are always looking for a formula or a pattern that we can utilize to make something work. We want something we can wrap our minds around and figure out. That is why it is so easy for us to gravitate toward religion. We like the rituals and routines of religion because we can understand it and control it. However, God's kingdom can't be understood with a worldly religious mind.

Jesus reveals their lack of understanding. He says if you simply had the smallest amount of what He possessed you wouldn't just be able to drive out this devil—you'd look at this mountain, say "move," and it would move. He said you don't have that kind of faith because you don't pray.

They were not yet men of persistent prayer and therefore they did not carry any authority on their lives. They failed to realize that when they went two by two they went out under Christ's authority. They were obeying His word and working underneath His authority. However, since that time they had not sought to foster a deeper relationship with the Lord that would produce a greater life of power and authority within them.

That was my problem that day in the restaurant. I was not yet a man of deep prayer and devotion with the Lord. I was on fire with initial flames of revival, but there was little depth to my life. I was still immature, lacking a bold faith. Thankfully, the Lord is patient with us, always instructing us and leading us toward maturity.

Jesus offers the disciples a solution. He says, "*This kind does not go out except by prayer and fasting.*" Prayer and fasting is the remedy for unbelief. They could not manifest deliverance because of a lack of prayer and fasting on their part.

Be careful here! Don't make the mistake of reading Jesus's words with a works-driven mentality. When we approach prayer and fasting this way we see it simply as a means to an end. We wrongfully conclude that time in prayer will automatically equal power from Heaven. Prayer is not about my *doing*, it's about my *being*.

The Christian life is about *being*. There is genuine freedom when you come to that realization! I don't spend time in prayer so that I can *do* the things Jesus did. I spend time in prayer so that I can *be* the person Jesus is. The more time I spend with Him, the more I become like Him. Signs and wonders follow as a secondary consequence of a life lived in Him. They are the witness that follow those who are truly in him (John 10:37-38).

Jesus encouraged His disciples to spend more time in prayer. A life lived within the secret place of prayer has ears that are in tune with the Father's voice. Prayer affects our *being* because prayer affects our *hearing*. The more you know the sound of His voice, the more confidence you place in His voice. Knowing God and being known by God are the purposes of prayer. Developing a trust in His voice and following His leading puts you in union with Him so that when you face great situations you face them with a great God. Simply put, prayer and fasting make you receptive to God's voice.

HELP MY UNBELIEF!

When Jesus intervenes in this situation, He isn't coming to the disciples' rescue. He responds to a father's desperation. It's the father who makes a confession that the double-minded can follow the example of. He says to Jesus, *"I believe, help my unbelief."*

I've prayed that prayer many times. "Jesus I believe in You, but help me to believe You! I know your word is true, help me to believe upon your truth. Forgive me for my unbelief. Give me the strength to face my fears and challenge my doubts. I don't want to be double-minded or tossed about anymore in my faith."

Have you found yourself there? Maybe you thought it was wrong to verbalize or even express your doubts and fears. To be honest, until we are willing to come to Jesus in openness and transparency we will remain stuck wondering why our faith remains immature and fruitless.

God is not afraid of your questions. In fact, asking the right questions is the best place to begin. Man-made religion teaches us to just ignore these things and keep doing the routine. They say, "Fake it until you make it." Christianity isn't a religion, it's a journey that we are sojourning on with a faithful teacher who is ready to lead and guide you into maturity (1 Peter 2:11; John 16:13).

The parable of the sower shows us that our faith can be restricted by our fear and doubt. These are two thorns that grow around us seeking to choke out our faith. Let's confront these two faith killers head-on and discover how you can push through them to find true faith.

FACING OUR FEARS

You've likely asked the *what if* question more than once. What if I'm wrong? What if my faith is not real? What if God doesn't exist? What if I try this and it doesn't work? What if I step out on the water and sink? What if I take a stand for my faith and fail? What if I speak up and I am mocked and ridiculed? What if I put myself out there and find out You're not there?

What if will play in our heads like a song stuck on repeat when we find ourselves in a moment of decision. The more difficult the decision the more repeated the questions. These questions are an expression of our fears. They are rooted in the worries and cares of this life. Fear thrives in a *what if* environment.

Pushing past our fears requires stirring up our faith. Paul, writing to his spiritual son Timothy, encourages him to face his fears and embrace faith in this way. He writes, "*I remember your genuine faith, for you share the faith that first filled your grandmother Lois and your mother, Eunice. And I know that same faith continues strong in you. This is why I remind you to fan into flames the spiritual gift God gave you when I laid my hands on you. For God has not given us a spirit of fear and timidity, but of power, love, and sound mind*" (2 Timothy 1:5-7).

Paul reminds Timothy of the faith he has watched grow within him over the years. It was handed down to him by a faith-filled grandmother and mother. He says stir it up! Fan it into flame. Pray in the Spirit and build up your faith. When you are in the Spirit, you are not in the environment of fear, but the environment of power and love, and there you have a sound mind. Paul says that he who prays in the Spirit "*edifies himself*" (1 Corinthians 14:14). That means you can build yourself up and encourage your own faith. If you want to step out of fear and into faith, get in the Spirit.

Remember James teaches us that when you are not of sound mind, but are double-minded, you're unstable in all your ways and will receive nothing from the Lord. A sound mind is a stable mind. The double-minded man is caught between two minds: fear and faith. Faith does not thrive in the *what if* environment that fear creates. Double mindedness causes us to be faithless and remain immature.

It's easy to think of fear as being the opposite of faith, but it's not. Fear *is* faith. Just as faith is the substance of things hoped for, fear is the substance of things dreaded. Faith is a deep belief that the positive thing I hope for will happen. Likewise fear is a deep belief that the negative thing that I dread is more likely to happen. Simply put, fear places a greater faith in the enemy than in the Lord.

Where you point your faith is the direction you'll head. Those who give into their fear and believe their doubts will find themselves experiencing exactly what they feared. Why? Because faith, whether positive or negative, always works.

Fear places greater faith in what you can and cannot do instead of what you believe God can do. In fact, fear is all about our abilities. In your head you may know that God can and does do the impossible, but in your heart you doubt that it will happen for you. Fear has greater faith in your ability, or lack thereof, than in God's ability.

Instead of asking *what if* it's time to start asking *what is.* Faith doesn't thrive in a *what if* environment. That is the domain of fear. Faith lives in a *what is* environment. When fear comes asking *what if,* turn the table on your fear and respond with what God says is!

What does God's word say about the situation you are facing? What verses can you turn to and meditate on throughout the day? What do you hear God saying to you right now? If God said it, then this is *what is.* His word is true and every other word or question is a lie. The word teaches us that "*faith comes by hearing, hearing by the word of God*" (Romans 10:17). When I hear God's word, I am hearing His unshakeable, unstoppable truth. There is not a single *what if* question that cannot be immediately silenced by what God says is. Face your fear with what is, and fear disappears.

This is why Jesus, when facing His test in the desert, said, "*Man does not live by bread alone, but every word that proceeds out of the mouth of God*" (Matthew 4:4). *Proceeds* is present tense. It's not just about what God has said, but what He is saying at this moment! This is why prayer and fasting is so important. It gets us in an environment where we can hear from the Lord. When I can hear His voice, I'll know *what is* and be able to challenge my fears with God's truth.

PUSHING THROUGH THE DOUBTS

Jesus made an incredible statement to the father. He said, *"Anything is possible to him who believes."* It is interesting that He didn't preface or restrict that. This bold statement is absolutely true. A man who fully believes something can accomplish anything he sets his faith toward. James shares the antithesis of this. He says that a man who doubts will receive nothing from the Lord. It is our belief that makes all things possible while our doubts make nothing possible.

When you endeavor to step out in faith, doubt will be the first thing to challenge it. We often express our uncertainty with questions that begin with, "I don't know..."

I don't know if this is actually true. I don't know if I can do this. I don't know if God will heal me. I don't know if God will come through for me.

I don't know is the expression of our doubts. These seeds of unbelief are sown within our minds and grow like weeds around our faith until it chokes the life out of us and kills off our fruit. Just as faith cannot thrive in an environment of fear, it also cannot live in the midst of unbelief.

Unbelief is the complete lack of faith. It is the opposite of faith. This is why unbelief is labeled in scripture as sin (John 16:9-19, Hebrews 3:12, Romans 14:23). Unbelief is the consequence of believing our doubts. When we say, "I don't know" we are expressing our uncertainty. Our doubts reveal how little we truly know God's word and His power. Jesus said that we are in error "*because you do not know the Scriptures or the power of God*" (Mark 12:14).

There is a big difference between knowing something in theory and knowing it in reality. Often times we consider knowledge to be the product of something learned in a classroom or read in a book. But true knowledge is the understanding gained from actual intimate interaction.

Jesus was addressing the error of the religious. They loved to debate scriptures and argue doctrine. They came to Jesus with their pointless quizzes hoping to engage Him in their religious games. Jesus called them out. He said, "You do not know the scriptures." This was insulting to the religious men who had spent most of their lives memorizing the text of Scripture. However, just because they knew the words didn't mean they knew the word. So true! Just because we know the words doesn't mean we *know the word!*

Churches have become skilled at filling the minds of their members with information about God. They teach the scriptures and deliver theories, but how many invite the hearers into an interactive encounter with God? Church is not supposed to be a place that educates us about Jesus. It's supposed to be a place where we encounter Jesus.

When God gave Moses the law, the people were not distant. They didn't receive God's word secondhand. They were there at the foot of the mountain. They saw the billowing smoke and lightning. They smelled the aroma of His presence. They felt the heat of His holy fire and heard the voice of God through the thunder as He said, "*I am the Lord your God*" (Exodus 20:2).

That interaction with God removed all doubt within God's people. Even when they rebelled against God, the kings and prophets would always point back to that moment and say, "You were there. You saw with your own eyes." That knowledge carried many of God's people through the generations. They couldn't doubt God because they had seen God.

This is how Jesus taught the multitudes as well. He performed miracles and then taught the people. His preaching came with a demonstration of power. The miracles testified to the validity of the word. They marveled at how Jesus taught so differently from the other teachers. Jesus taught with authority and His words worked. They had an interaction with the word.

Paul followed the same example. He said, "*My speech and my preaching were not with persuasive words of human wisdom, but in demonstration of the Spirit and of power, that your faith should not be in the wisdom of men but in the power of God*" (1 Corinthians 2:4-5).

When our faith is based on pure intellect alone we find ourselves in error. But when the truth of the scripture finds its way into our hearts and we have experienced the power of God, all doubts are removed. This is the joy of much fasting and prayer. We are invited to have an encounter with the living God. We no longer have to doubt Him, because we know Him.

The father said to Jesus, *"I believe."* He had a measure of faith in Jesus to perform miracles. He knew Jesus carried authority. He sought to know Jesus more when he said, *"Help my unbelief"* (Mark 9:24). You and I can know the same blessed place. You already have a measure of faith in Jesus. I encourage you to set time aside for fasting and praying. Ask Him to help your unbelief. I have no doubt you will find a glorious encounter with Him that challenges your fear and sets aside your doubt.

> *Lord I believe in You; help me now to believe Your word. Teach me to put faith in Your voice so that I might face my own fears and silence my doubts. All things are possible to me if I just believe. Help me to believe!*

Chapter Six

Receptivity

Cultivating a spirit that is receptive to the word of God

"But the seed on good soil stands for those with a noble and good heart, who hear the word, retain it, and by persevering produce a crop."
— LUKE 8:15, NIV

As we've been following the parable of the sower we now come to the final soil presented by Jesus: the receptive one. This soil is likened to those with a noble and good heart who not only hear His word, they retain the word, and produce a great harvest from the word. Yes, this can be viewed as the man who has been reborn into the kingdom of God, but as we have discovered, the principle does not stop there. The desire of a true disciple is to become fully receptive to every word that the Father sows, understanding that they are not only the words of salvation, but the very words of life itself.

Peter writes, *"Grace and peace be multiplied to you in the knowledge of God and of Jesus our Lord, as His divine power has given to us all things that pertain to life and godliness, through the knowledge of Him who called us by glory and virtue, by which have been given to us exceedingly great and precious promises, that through these you may be partakers of the divine nature, having escaped the corruption that is in the world through lust"* (1 Peter 1:2-4).

Everything you need is found in Christ. Everything means everything. I don't have to look elsewhere. Whatever I need is already provided by Him. Peter says that *"all things that pertain to life and godliness"* are supplied in Christ. Not just our spiritual needs, but everything we need for life as well. This is why Jesus could follow the Spirit into a desert without making any provision for food or drink. He was nourished by food *"of which you do not know"* (John 4:32). He lived off the very words that came from His Father's mouth and not bread alone.

We too can know the supernatural nourishment that comes from feasting daily at His table upon His very words, those written in His book and spoken through the Spirit. This is what it means to be *"partakers of the divine nature."* It's called receptivity.

This is why we must allow the Holy Spirit to break the fallow ground. The reason why we welcome trials and tests is to reveal the rocks and shallow depths of our faith so that our faith will grow and mature. It is why the weeds and thorns of our fears and doubts must be pulled out by the roots. All these things prepare the ground for the seed. They make us receptive. The more receptive the soil the more fruit the seed will bear. If we do our part, the seed does its part! Everything the Lord has brought into our life thus far has been worth it. Now we are ready to be shaped and molded into a vessel of honor befitting His glory!

Becoming a Receptive Vessel

Sitting in my office is an extraordinary piece of pottery that is really more of a sculpted work of art than it is a vase. It was a gift from a master potter. He gave it to me after we had spent several days together working in his studio. I wanted to learn more about the process of taking clay and sculpting it into a piece of pottery. Much like the prophet Jeremiah, I went to the potter's house.

While I write these words I am looking at this beautiful yet brutal masterpiece. As a vessel, it is useless—there is a gash on its side that would immediately spill out whatever it is filled with. That open wound wasn't a mistake—this piece wasn't created to be poured into, it was made to be poured out of.

The pot is shaped like a human torso. The base of the pot forms the waist; the top stops at the neck. It is marred across the top and back with what looks like the welts and rips you'd expect to see from a severe flogging. On its right side is a punctured hole. Each of these violent marks were skillfully and willfully placed there by the potter himself.

I was there that day as a witness when he first shaped it from a simple lump of clay. I watched as he prepared this earthen medium on his bench. He began by forcefully kneading it over and over again with the strength of his hands and the weight of his upper body. This process was necessary to ensure that the clay was brought into perfect uniformity and was the right quality. It had to be free of contaminates and perfectly yielded to the master's hands. Once he was satisfied that the clay was ready, he then threw it onto the wheel. There the clay, the wheel, and the potter began to work together as one, like a well-rehearsed ballet.

When his wheel came to rest, the piece was exquisite in form but the potter wasn't done. Using his hands he shaped the pot into the form of a human body from the waist to the neck. I had never seen anything quite like it before. It was truly something to behold. It was a masterpiece.

However, the creator was not done. The potter now took a blade and began to scar the pot. It was offensive to watch this thing of beauty be bruised in such a way. I wondered how an artist who took great pride in his work could now destroy something so unique.

Every piece of pottery has a specific purpose that was predetermined by its creator. The clay doesn't say to the potter, "I would like to be a glorious vase or a fine piece of china fit for a royal palace." The potter is the one who decides what the clay will become. He is the one who creates it. He assigns its purpose and it is he who determines its value.

As I watched in horror, he then took the blade and pierced its side. Then, with his own hands, he opened the wound. This final scar would forever ensure that anything poured in would be freely poured out. Like I mentioned before, it wasn't made to contain, but to release.

Finally, the piece was finished. The potter was fully satisfied. He now left the pot to rest for several days after which it would be placed into a fire to be transformed from brittle clay to the hardened vessel that now sits by my desk. Though it is not useful as a vessel, it is a powerful message as it silently, yet boldly, preaches the cross of Christ.

The imagery of the potter and the clay is familiar in scripture. It is a potent metaphor for our relationship with our Creator. My time with this master potter gave me a greater appreciation for the process and a better revelation of what it means to be yielded to our Creator's hands, fully receptive to His work within us.

This is why the prophet Jeremiah was instructed to go to the potter's house. It was there the Lord revealed to him how He was at work shaping His people just as a potter shapes clay. Similarly Isaiah echoed, "*We are the clay, and You our potter; and all we are the work of Your hand*" (Isaiah 64:8). Even Paul writes, "*We have this treasure in earthen vessels [jars of clay], that the excellence of the power may be of God and not of us*" (2 Corinthians 4:7).

The message is clear. God is the master potter and even now He is at work, shaping each of us into vessels of honor. Our job is incredibly simple. We must yield to the Master's hands. Unfortunately that is easier said than done.

You have already been engaged in this process longer than you realize. David wrote, "*For You formed my inward parts; you covered me in my mother's womb. I will praise You, for I am fearfully and wonderfully made; marvelous are Your works, and that my soul knows very well. My frame was not hidden from You, when I was made in secret, and skillfully wrought in the lowest parts of the earth. Your eyes saw my substance, being yet unformed. And in Your book they all were written, the days fashioned for me, when as yet there were none of them*" (Psalm 139:13-16).

David's inspired words paint a magnificent image of the Master's initial work in us from within our mother's womb. God was already shaping our lives according to His plans and purposes before we drew our first breath. He hasn't just been working with you as of late—He's been at work from the very beginning. There should be no doubt that He has a plan and purpose for you already and He is at work to accomplish His will within you.

"'For I know the plans I have for you,' declares the Lord, 'plans to prosper you and not to harm you, plans to give you hope and a future'" (Jeremiah 29:11). He said I have *"plans"* not *"a plan."* Before He formed you in the womb, He knew you and began to dream about you. David tells us that He wrote down each and every one of those days before a single one of them came into being. As unbelievable as it is, God knew every one of your days before you experienced your first one. Yes, both the good days and the bad days.

You may be thinking about some of those bad days you've experienced wondering how God could have ever allowed that to take place. Those days may have come as the consequence of your own bad decisions or could have been brought on by the decisions of others. Though no one could ever offer a simple answer for some of your darkest days, I can assure you that though God foresaw it, it wasn't His original dream for you.

How can I be so sure of this? One need only look at God's original creation in the Garden of Eden. There, God shaped man and woman in perfection from the earth. He placed them within a well-prepared garden and provided everything they needed. There was no sickness, no pain, and no death. Adam walked with God, enjoying the wonder of His creation and the awesomeness of His presence. It was man who chose to walk away and bring the curse into creation. The curse was not God's plan. It was the result of man's rebellion. Every bad day and every dark situation you have endured can be traced back to that day when Adam and Eve first sinned against God. Thankfully, God did not leave us in that fallen, broken condition. He is able to use what is bruised and broken to recreate within us His plan and purpose.

The enemy also has a plan for your life. He desires to kill, steal, and destroy you (John 10:10). However, even when the enemy comes to destroy, you can rest assured that what he does to harm you, God can and will turn for your good if you will trust Him.

Nothing takes place in our lives that isn't Father filtered. God will allow the enemy to test us, or allow the natural consequence of our choices to overcome us. He does so not to destroy us, but to draw us. As Paul says so well, "*And we know that all things work together for good to those who love God, to those who are the called according to His purpose*" (Romans 8:28).

God in His sovereignty has a unique way of using what seems painful one day to produce something beautiful the next. Joseph was imprisoned in Egypt so that one day he could govern Egypt. David was chased from the palace as a fugitive so that he could return one day as a king. Paul was blinded one day so that he would finally see Jesus. Trust me, God will use the darkest day in your life to bring you into a good and glorious day very soon.

God has a plan and purpose not only for your life—He has a plan for today. David said that God has already thought about this day and every day, from the beginning. You need to realize there isn't just a plan for my life, there is a plan for today!

We tend to miss the present because we constantly obsess about the whole. We think about the big picture for our lives, wondering what the finished project will be. In doing so we forfeit the present plan. We miss out on many of the wonders that could be discovered right here in this moment of this day. We miss so much that we could be experiencing in Him and with Him if we would just let Him work within us at this moment.

David said, "*How precious also are Your thoughts to me, O God! How great is the sum of them! If I should count them, they would be more in number than the sand*" (Psalm 139:17-18).

Even now the Lord has His hands in the clay of your life. He is moving through your dirt working to make you receptive to His purpose for your life. The Lord has more in mind than you could ever dream. Not only for your whole life, but for today as well. The key to realizing the fullness of everything God intends is found in our yielding to Him and becoming fully pliable for Him to shape us into the vessel of honor He desires. Being receptive to everything God has for you requires three things; learning to yield, trusting, and listening.

YIELDING!

As I mentioned, the process of making a clay vessel begins before the clay ever finds itself upon the wheel. This is the preparation stage. Though it is not glamorous, it is no less important.

The potter I worked with actually preferred to bypass store-bought clay for the clay you had to go out to find. He knew his region well and knew of an obscure location alongside a river where he could go and excavate his clay. He would select and cut the clay away from the earth.

I found this so interesting especially since I considered this real-life experience an eye opener into how we are the clay and Christ is the potter. Think about the way Jesus called His first disciples to Himself alongside the water's edge. Peter was used to being in the water fishing for fish, but Jesus called him away from that water to go fish for men. He extracted him out of an earthly kingdom and brought him into a heavenly kingdom.

He told them, "*You didn't choose me, I chose you*" (John 15:16). Just like He chose you. He was the one who called, and you simply answered. The day you surrendered your life to

Jesus and confessed Him as Lord was the first day that you started to yield to His hand. That day He cut you away from the world, and the process of preparation began.

The potter brought the clay back to his studio and placed it upon his worktable to prepare it. The preparation was thorough and forceful. The clay had to be free of contaminates and brought into uniformity. He worked it over and over until it was pure and pliable. I learned that clay doesn't come out of the earth ready to be shaped—it resists it, but as the potter wedges the clay time and time again, eventually it surrenders. Until it surrenders, it cannot be placed upon the wheel.

Do you get this? There are multiple times in our lives that we are in seasons of preparation. These times can be painful and humiliating. We feel the weight bearing down around us forcing us to our knees. We experience the pain that comes as things are uprooted and removed from our lives. We pray for it to stop, but fail to realize that the Lord is at work. Though the process cannot be omitted it can be accelerated if we would stop resisting and start submitting to the Lord.

We don't realize how much we resist and inhibit the Lord's work. We celebrate our own strength to manage whatever situation we face. My friend your strength is your weakness. The sooner you realize it, the better. This is why the Lord says, "*My grace is sufficient for you, for My strength is made perfect in weakness*" (2 Corinthians 12:9).

If you want to become receptive, it's imperative that you learn to yield! True humility can only be found when we finally recognize that He is in control and surrender everything to Him, holding nothing back. Everything that we are and everything that we have is His to do with as He pleases.

It is in this place of yielding where the fallowed ground is plowed and the rocks and weeds are removed. The kneading on the table prepares the soil to become receptive. Many remain on the master's table because they refuse to yield. They fight, but He is patient and continues to work over and over until they finally surrender.

Jesus said, "*Blessed are the poor in spirit for theirs is the kingdom of God*" (Matthew 5:3). To be found spiritually poor is a blessed place to be. Finding everything in God's kingdom and becoming a partner of His nature requires surrendering everything from ourselves. It is all stripped away. The Lord is your all in all. There is no other option. To the world, and even to some Christians, it looks like giving up and for some that is the point we have to be taken to. However the reality of this poverty of spirit means we've finally come to the end of ourselves and completely given God our all.

Have you found this place? Don't be so quick to assume you have. Yielding isn't easy—we are more resistant than we realize.

Are there repetitive habits, thoughts, or mentalities that you still wrestle with? Is there something you constantly debate with yourself and others as to whether or not it is sin? Why not just call it sin, remove it from your life, and move on? Where do you continue to rebel against the Lord? Do you compare yourself to others? Find it easy to judge another believer? Do your ears turn to or away from gossip? When criticism comes your way do you get offended? Are you quick to defend yourself or quick to justify or rationalize a situation? Do you find yourself repeating the same mistakes? Do you seem to keep going through the same situations? The human heart is deceptive and rebellious by nature—it doesn't humble itself without a fight!

Where do you reserve things for yourself? What would hurt the most to be taken away from you right now? If God doesn't come through for you in a situation where are you going to turn to next? What is your backup plan? The poor in spirit have no backup plan and nothing to lose.

Trust me, God is at work right now in your life for your good and His glory. He knows the plans He has for you. There is nothing that takes place in your life that has caught Him by surprise. Everything that comes your way is allowed for a reason. We will either be humbled or be humiliated—God will use either to bring us to a point where we become yielded and made ready to move onto His wheel and be formed.

TRUSTING!

The next step in forming pottery is called "throwing the pot." This is where the prepared clay is placed upon the wheel, centered, and pulled up. The clay comes off the master's table and lands with force upon the wheel. The reason it is done with such force is so that the clay adheres to the wheel. Things are about to begin to turn in the life of the clay and it has to hold fast to the wheel and not get spun off.

What a picture of true New Testament belief! Belief means to adhere to something like glue. There is no wavering, no separating us from the Master. Go ahead, let the world around us spin out of control. Our faith is in Him and cannot be shaken. We can trust the Master's hands.

As the wheel begins to spin the potter starts to center the clay. Once again the clay has to learn to be submitted to the potter. He places his hands around the clay and spins it until it becomes uniform and in perfect union with the wheel. Without this, the clay would be unbalanced and unable to be formed.

Watching the clay and potter work together as one, I think of Jesus as He says, *"I and my Father are one"* (John 10:30). He could only do and say what the Father is doing and saying. They were in harmony with one another. Jesus is joined to the Father are just as we are joined to His Son. In Him we live and move and have our being.

Once the pot is centered, it is time to be opened up. The potter places his hand onto the clay and pushes into it—suddenly the clay transforms and now begins to look like a vessel. It is shallow at first, but as the wheel spins, the sides begin to be pulled up. They climb higher and higher as the pot takes shape. This is the most beautiful part of the process to watch.

No doubt you can remember those points in your life where you experienced spiritual growth spurts. Each day comes with a greater level of joy and anticipation. I experienced this when I first surrendered my life to Christ. For two weeks I woke up early each morning at five a.m. and began to pray. It came without effort. I was excited to share my faith with anyone willing to listen. It happened again when I enrolled in Bible school. For two years I experienced incredible growth and transformation as I dove deeper into the word. This past year I have experienced seasons of exponential growth. There is nothing quite like being on the Master's wheel and trusting the work of His hands!

LISTENING!

Once the pot is fully formed, it is removed from the wheel and allowed to sit for a season. For weeks it is left alone to dry. What began with such activity is now incredibly still. This time is necessary to prepare the pot for the final stage when it will be placed into the fire.

You could liken it to the wilderness—a time period that many flee, but is a blessed time that must be embraced. Moses found his purpose in the wilderness. The nation of Israel was extracted from Egypt and brought into the wilderness. Elijah retreated to the wilderness, and Elisha received his mantle in the wilderness. David became a man after God's own heart in the remote regions of his wilderness. Jesus was driven by the Spirit out into the wilderness.

There is a wilderness experience coming for you as well when you are allowed to sit. It may seem that much isn't taking place on the outside, and it's not. What is happening is taking place within. The previous work of the Master's hands is setting itself up within you. During this process the clay is at its most fragile point and must be handled with the utmost care. Thankfully the Master has the most caring hands.

I used to run from these places, but I've now learned the value of them. There are things you can learn and receive in the wilderness that cannot come from anywhere else. The wilderness is a part of the listening process. The first time I fully yielded to my wilderness experience, I chose to go to our church and sit in the sanctuary for hours in silence listening. I sat for two weeks. Some may think that was a waste of time, but on that fourteenth day, I began to hear His voice with such clarity that I wrote pages that have sustained me to this day. In fact this book came out of that time.

You don't plant a seed and see it immediately grow. It has to have a season of death, buried beneath the surface in waiting. We need to learn to sit in waiting within our wilderness. There the word of the Lord comes to sustain us. We learn to listen and hear Him with a greater clarity. This is where we truly become receptive.

People perish because they don't know God's word or His power. They refuse to listen to God's word and His voice. What a shame, because everything they need is found in Him.

Are you getting this yet? Here we are halfway through this book and already enough scriptural truth has been shared to forever change your life. Have you had ears to hear it? What situations and circumstances are you currently facing? What are you believing for? Are you seeing the fullness of God's promises in the midst of those situations?

Do you realize that everything you need is found in Him and in His word? Do you realize that if you would simply be receptive to His word, you would start to bear fruit according to that word? Let he who has ears to hear, let him hear!

The Bible is a radical book. It is filled with bold stories and even bolder promises. All of God's promises are certain. It's not a matter of it working for one person and not another. Some believers walk into the fullness of God's promises, while many remain without. The difference is one is receptive and the other is not.

Jesus made a bold statement when He said, "*If you can believe, all things are possible to him who believes*" (Mark 9:23). What a promise! All things are possible. Paul said it this way, "*I can do all things through Christ who strengthens me*" (Philippians 4:13). The only condition Jesus gives is to simply believe His words.

Let's discuss a few wilderness experiences you may be in the midst of in your life right now.

Perhaps you are facing the wilderness concerning your finances. You've been laid off and out of work for some time. Maybe you are looking for a new job or just feel stuck. You may be covered up in debt or enslaved to a bank or a credit card.

Those with an unreceptive soil face this wilderness this way. The hardened soil says, "I don't have time to listen to you. I don't have time to pray or read God's word. I'm doing everything I can just to stay above water. I need to focus on me right now, I'll deal with God later."

That's the problem. Don't start with you, start with God. If you'd simply listen and be receptive to God's word you'd see your way out.

The rocky soil says, "I knew sooner or later he would start talking about money. That's all these preachers ever talk about. Money, money, money. I know all this already. I've heard it before. Give to God. Trust God, He will take care of me."

There is such a difference between the facts we can regurgitate and the beliefs we hold in our hearts. This person knows what the word says, but doesn't really believe it. Behavior bears out belief! If you really believed it, you'd be doing it.

The thorny soil says, "I know God's word is true, but I'm finding it so hard to trust right now. I don't know how I'm going to pay my bills. I want to believe, but my doubts are killing my belief."

Not one of these *soils* can expect to see any fruit from God's word. The hardness of their hearts, the trials and tests and the doubts are keeping them from being receptive and receiving the promises that is prophesied in God's word.

Listen to what God's word says:

> *You will again obey the LORD and follow all His commands I am giving you today. Then the LORD your God will make you most prosperous in all the work of your hands.* (Deuteronomy 30:8-9)

> *Give, and it will be given to you. A good measure, pressed down, shaken together and running over, will be poured into your lap. For with the measure*

> *you use, it will be measured to you.* (Luke 6:38, NIV)

The receptive ear hears these promises and believes them. They let the seeds of these truths go deep into their hearts and hold on to them. They refuse to let doubt and fear take them away. The receptive simply believe and see the impossible become possible!

Your wilderness may be more physical. Perhaps you are sick right now, facing a medical issue that the doctors give little hope for. The unreceptive discount God's healing power. They have made up their mind that God doesn't heal anymore. Others believe God *can* heal, but they doubt that He *has* healed them. Then there are those who know the theology of healing, but don't know the power of healing. People don't get healed because they have theology, they get healed because they have faith!

Do you need a healing? Open your ears and let these words go through you!

> *Praise the LORD, O my soul; all my inmost being, praise His holy name. Praise the LORD, O my soul, and forget not all His benefits—who forgives all your sins and heals all your diseases.* (Psalm 103:1-3)

> *Is anyone among you sick? Let him call for the elders of the church, and let them pray over him, anointing him with oil in the name of the Lord. And the prayer of faith will save the sick, and the Lord will raise him up.* (James 5:14-15)

> *Now this is the confidence that we have in Him, that if we ask anything according to His will, He hears us. And if we know that He hears us, whatever we*

> *ask, we know that we have the petitions that we have asked of Him.* (1 John 5:14-15)

> *So Jesus said to them, "If you have faith as a mustard seed, you will say to this mountain, 'Move from here to there,' and it will move; and nothing will be impossible for you."* (Matthew 17:20)

> *Assuredly, I say to you, whatever you bind on earth will be bound in heaven, and whatever you loose on earth will be loosed in heaven. Again I say to you that if two of you agree on earth concerning anything that they ask, it will be done for them by My Father in heaven. For where two or three are gathered together in My name, I am there in the midst of them.* (Matthew 18:18-20)

Maybe your wilderness is more spiritual. You could be lost in the world, backslidden or running away from God. The hard-hearted instantly reject the word of God the moment they hear it. The shallow religious believer will try to debate it until they kill it. The double-minded individual allows their unbelief to choke out their spiritual life. But not you. I have to believe if you are currently away from God and have made it to this point right now, you are opening your ears to your Savior! You are becoming receptive to His voice. He's been patient with you. Listen to this:

> *The Lord is not slow in keeping his promise, as some understand slowness. He is patient with you, not wanting anyone to perish, but everyone to come to repentance.* (2 Peter 3:9)

> *Behold, I stand at the door and knock. If anyone hears My voice and opens the door, I will come in to*

> *him and dine with him, and he with Me.* (Revelation 3:20)
>
> *For, "whoever calls on the name of the Lord shall be saved."* (Romans 10:13)

If that is you, call on His name right now! Say the name "Jesus" and let Him come flood the space you are sitting in.

Another wilderness, the one that I knew for eighteen years of my life, was one of religion. There was no life in the church and no life in me. Then revival showed up! Revival is when you become fully alive in God. It is awakening to His Spirit and life. Many are resistant to revival. They hold fast to their plans and programs and have no need for His presence. You can sow the seeds of revival upon them, but it will not penetrate their hardened hearts. Others see revival as a thing that comes and goes. It is a series of meetings that takes place within a building. They don't realize that revival is a meeting that takes place within your heart. Still others resist revival because they refuse to repent. They don't want to embrace holiness within their lives. They want a carnal Christianity. But if your heart burns for revival let these revival seeds find the receptive soil of your heart.

> *And these signs will follow those who believe: In My name they will cast out demons; they will speak with new tongues; they will take up serpents; and if they drink anything deadly, it will by no means hurt them; they will lay hands on the sick, and they will recover.* (Mark 16:17-18)
>
> *But you shall receive power when the Holy Spirit has come upon you; and you shall be witnesses to Me in Jerusalem, and in all Judea and Samaria, and to the end of the earth.* (Acts 1:8)

> *Then Peter said to them, "Repent, and let every one of you be baptized in the name of Jesus Christ for the remission of sins; and you shall receive the gift of the Holy Spirit. For the promise is to you and to your children, and to all who are afar off, as many as the Lord our God will call."* (Acts 2:38-39)

> *Therefore I remind you to stir up the gift of God which is in you through the laying on of my hands. For God has not given us a spirit of fear, but of power and of love and of a sound mind.* (2 Timothy 1:6-7)

If you found it easy to read through or skip over those scriptures I challenge the receptivity of your heart. It is no wonder those very words that offer life are not bringing forth life within you—you refuse to listen. If you are in one of those wildernesses those words were like finding a spring in the desert. Don't just refresh yourself and then move on. Stay! Park yourself at that spring and begin to meditate on His words. Let them get deep within you. You're learning to listen!

The wilderness is a necessary part of the process. Though it takes time to still ourselves and listen, it is worth it. How can I have faith if I'm not hearing? How can I hear if I'm not listening?

The wilderness takes time, but it will not last forever. It is an important part of the process that cannot be rushed. Though it can't be accelerated, it can be lengthened. Learning to yield, trust, and listen during this season will ensure you stay as long as necessary, but not a day longer than was needed.

GETTING IN THE FIRE

When the pot has sat long enough it is now ready for the fire. Here it is super-heated and the structure of the pot changes. It will never be the same after the fire. A transformation will take place and the clay will never be able to return to the earth it came from. The pot will go through two fires. The first firing will harden the pot and remove all impurities. The second firing is to seal it so that it may hold what is poured in.

Jesus is celebrating His last Passover meal with the disciples when He reveals to Peter that "*Satan has asked for you, that he may sift you as wheat*" (Luke 22:31). This is not a prophetic word that most of us would get excited about. Perhaps Peter was hoping the next words out of Jesus's mouth would be, "but I have stopped him from doing so." However, that is not what Peter hears. Jesus says, "*But I have prayed for you, that your faith should not fail; and when you have returned to Me, strengthen your brethren*" (Luke 22:32).

Peter was on his way to the fire. He was about to be placed into a test that would shake him to his core. Interesting that Jesus didn't stop the fire—He allowed it. Why? Because it was necessary. Peter would return transformed and able to be a strength to his brothers in Jesus's absence. This was Peter's first fire; the second came on the Day of Pentecost when he was baptized in Holy Spirit and fire. That fire forever set Peter apart. The man who days before cowered in fear and denied Jesus stood with boldness before thousands and declared Jesus. What a difference the fire makes!

The master potter took the pot through two fires: the first to reveal it, the second to seal it. This is why James tells us to celebrate the trials and tests of our faith because they cause our faith to mature through perseverance. Jesus said that the final soil, the receptive soil, produces a multiplied harvest through perseverance. The fire hardens our faith.

Jesus comes to baptize us in Holy Spirit and in fire. The fire is necessary! The second fire, the fire of the Holy Ghost, seals us and sets us apart. It empowers us to be a witness. It transforms us from an empty vessel to a vessel overflowing with the presence of the Lord. If you have not yet experienced this fire, call out to Him—shut yourself up in a room and wait until you have been endued with power from on high.

Lord, set me ablaze with the fire of the Holy Ghost. Baptize me in Your Spirit. I yield my life to You and fully trust Your activity in my life. My ears are open and I am finally listening. Speak to me.

Chapter Seven

A Made-Up Mind

There is power in a made-up mind... if it's made up in the right things

"Jesus said to him, 'If you can believe, all things are possible to him who believes.'"
—MARK 9:23, NIV

It was late spring in 2011 and I was sitting beneath three towering crosses that stand along the side of Interstate 10 in Baton Rouge, Louisiana. I had just received a phone call asking me to get back to Dallas immediately. Doctors had placed my friend, mentor, and spiritual father Steve Hill under the care of hospice and given him a few hours to live.

Steve's health was fully depleted after four long years of battling melanoma and enduring the devastating side effects of the various treatments he had undergone. He had been at death's door several times over the past four years.

Miraculously Steve would always bounce back. However, this time was different, we all knew it. Medically he was out of options and out of time. It was over.

When I heard the news I immediately went to the prayer garden that sat in the shadow of these three crosses. My heart was heavy. With more tears than words I cried out to God. I had known that Steve's breakthrough would not come at the hands of doctors. God wasn't going to share the credit for touching his body with anyone. Now that the doctors were finally through, this was fully in God's hands. That day as I prayed in the garden I felt God's peace. I knew He was about to move in the most extraordinary way. I took a picture from the garden, looking up at the center cross, the sun perfectly positioned behind the intersection of the two beams. I wanted a reminder of this day, the day that everything changed.

Arriving back in Dallas and walking into the room where Steve was lying on a hospital bed was a sobering moment. It is impossible to convey the hopelessness of the situation that stood before us. We had stood in faith with Steve for four long years expecting to see him emerge victorious from this fight. Now, everything said this was the end. His body lay there like a pale, lifeless corpse. There was hardly a sign of life in him. Nearly all of his organs had already shut down. He was barely breathing. You expected any second would be his last. We were against hope, but still had hope. Man had done all that he could and now we were in the domain of what God could do.

Steve's last prayer before drifting off into the abyss of darkness was that Jesus would raise him up and give him the opportunity to win one million more souls for the kingdom. Naturally speaking that prayer was going to go unanswered.

Steve had lived a miraculous life. He was twenty-one years of age when he experienced a radical conversion. He called on the name of Jesus from the violent convulsions of a heroin overdose. Within thirty seconds he was completely set free. He never looked back. Later he and his wife Jeri set out to Argentina, Spain, and Russia, planting churches and spreading revival everywhere they stepped. Then God used Steve on Father's Day of 1995 to spark revival in a church in Pensacola, Florida, that lasted 5 years, attracted over 4 million people and won over 150,000 people to the Lord.

Steve was never one to rest on yesterday's triumphs. He would tell me, "Daniel that is what God did, not what He is doing." Always pushing for more souls, he and Jeri planted a church in Dallas in 2003 and a school of ministry in 2004 that sent dozens of world changers into the far reaches of the earth. In 2006 Steve re-launched his evangelistic ministry and began traveling all over the world and broadcasting evangelistic messages to millions. That was when the greatest attack on his life took place. Like a good solider, Steve pushed through, but it became obvious that the cancer and the subsequent treatments were taking a toll on him and the ministry. Steve was unable to provide the oversight and leadership input that was necessary to position these ministries to move forward. Four years had passed and the melanoma was now threatening to leave all of these last works in disarray.

Steve sought to live his life in a manner reflective of the apostle Paul. His greatest desire was to serve God to the fullest and finish the work the Lord had assigned to him to do. That way one day he could cross the finish line and say like Paul, "*I have fought the good fight, I have finished the race, I have kept the faith*" (2 Timothy 4:7). Though Steve's body was finished, the work was not. That is why he prayed asking for more time.

We stood with Steve where his faith was. Millions of prayers began to bombard Heaven from thousands of people around the world. The church in Dallas called special prayer services to lift Steve up. There was a small but powerful group of our college students who took up the call to contend for Steve's healing. They came to the church every night at nine p.m. and joined hands in Steve's parking space at the church and prayed for at least an hour.

The prayer of faith works! We watched those few hours Steve was given stretch out to days. Then the days became weeks. One month after Steve was given up for dead, he woke up from his comatose-like state and began to interact with us for the first time. I was there that afternoon, totally astonished as Steve was able to share what the past month had been like. He said he felt like a prisoner in his own body. I spoke with a doctor who stood at Steve's side that day. He said there was absolutely no medical explanation for what was taking place. We were witnessing a bona fide miracle.

Steve shouldn't have been improving, yet he did. For nine months he got stronger and stronger. It wasn't an easy time, especially not for Jeri. She was with him every moment of every day. She wasn't just his helpmate, she was his primary caregiver. She showed us all what it looks like to stand with someone for better and for worse. Of all our prayers, her prayers and the prayers of the family spoke the loudest before God.

Then, in November 2011, the miracle came. Steve fully woke up from his "dark night of the soul." The darkness that had clouded his mind lifted, and the man of God we all knew came back.

The Lord miraculously gave Steve three additional years of life. During that time he was able to bring his leadership to the church and ministry. He personally installed his successor within the church he planted, raised up a Timothy to carry on part of his work, wrote two books, taped thirty new broadcasts, and pioneered ongoing outreaches into Africa and the Middle East. Those three additional years were incredibly productive. They have allowed Steve's legacy to endure. Before November 2011 none of this was possible. Thankfully there was a number of people around Steve with made-up minds to see him finish the work he was given to do. My friends, there is power in a made-up mind!

Keep a Closed Mind

> *God who gives life to the dead and calls into being things that were not. Against all hope, Abraham in hope believed and so became the father of many nations, just as it had been said to him.* (Romans 4:17-18)

Those words are more real to me today than at any other point in my life. I watched with my own eyes as God brought life back to what was dead. We were witnesses as God made divinely possible what was naturally impossible. Against all hope, in hope we believed.

Each of us will face those times when we stare off into the impossibilities of situations and circumstances. You've come to the end of everything you know to do and all that you trusted is now lost. For Abraham all he had was a promise from God that he would father a son who would be the first born of an entire nation. This was a natural impossibility.

When Abraham was faced with those facts, the Bible says that "*without weakening in his faith, he faced the fact that his body was as good as dead—since he was about a hundred years old—and that Sarah's womb was also dead. Yet he did not waver through unbelief regarding the promise of God, but was strengthened in his faith and gave glory to God, being fully persuaded that God had power to do what He had promised*" (Romans 4:19-21).

God's truth is greater than our facts! Abraham didn't deny the natural facts—he faced them. He just trusted that God's promised destiny superseded his present reality. He hoped against all hope. There was nothing in the natural that made sense. He had every reason to doubt, yet he didn't. He believed. His mind was made up. God's eternal truth was greater than the temporal facts.

There is incredible power in a made-up mind...if that mind is made up in the right things. A double-minded man is unstable in all his ways. It receives nothing from the Lord. However, a made-up mind is the springboard for all the glorious possibilities of the Lord. The key to receptivity is found in having a made-up mind.

A made-up mind is contrary to the popular philosophy of the world we live in. Open-mindedness is embraced as our culture's sole virtue. We are told truth is relative to the individual and nothing can ever be absolute. All thoughts and ideas must be tolerated as being equally true. Open-mindedness is encouraged at all times and toward all things and those who would hold to truth being absolute for all people at all times are outcasts.

There are a multitude of things that I do not know, and I am very much open-minded to learning about them. I love the art of discovery as all God's children should. However, sooner or later your path of discovery has to lead you to a place of decision. There comes a time to decide what is and is not true.

I have made up my mind on many things. Concerning gravity, I've made up my mind. What goes up will come back down. Concerning tomorrow I've made up my mind. The sun will rise at its appointed time. Some things are certain! The greatest of these certainties is the reality of God. Concerning Him, I've made up my mind; He is! I know this because I have personally encountered His presence and can now testify of that which I have seen with my eyes and heard with my ears. I have tasted and seen that the Lord is good. There are no doubts in what I experienced. My faith is set. My mind is made up.

God's truth is absolute. It has never and will never change. Like Him, it is the same yesterday, today, and forever. When everything else has passed away, His truth will remain. God's word is true, we either believe it or not; each of us must make up our mind concerning it.

Hebrews 11:6 states, "*Without faith it is impossible to please* [God], *for he who comes to God must believe that He is, and that He is a rewarder of those who diligently seek Him.*" Coming to God first requires a made-up mind concerning His reality. Those with faith will see Him; those without will not.

Truth must be settled within your mind. Without it you have no foundation on which to stand. Those who cannot embrace truth flounder. Those who make up their minds upon truth can stand. The world calls this being closed-minded—if so, then I am guilty as charged. There are things that I know to be true and you cannot change my mind about those things.

Those with made-up minds are in good company. Jesus was the most closed-minded individual to have ever walked the earth. He didn't walk in the middle of the road. He lived to the furthest extreme of truth. There was no persuading and no debating with Him. His mind was firmly set upon truth and He was unwavering. His perspective needed no correction. He saw things the way the Father saw them, and did things the way the Father did them. His mind was fully made up and with His mind set He did the impossible—He changed the world.

He spoke truth and calls us to make up our mind concerning it. His truth is not restrictive. He said, "*You shall know the truth and truth will set you free*" (John 8:32). His truth is freedom. I will always endeavor to be open-minded to His truth. I have not fully grasped it and certainly do not fully understand it, but I've made up my mind concerning the validity of it. Such a made-up mind is positioned to soar into the infinite possibilities of God.

This is the life of faith that the world will never understand. They say, "I will believe it when I see it." This thinking will never see anything. The multitudes watched Jesus perform miracles but refused to believe what they saw. True faith believes it, then sees it. This is a way of life for the believer. Faith is a certainty for us. We are certain of what cannot be seen. This is backward thinking to the naturally minded. They call it blind faith. How wrong they are.

Faith doesn't see, it hears! As it says, "*Faith comes by hearing, and hearing by the word of God*" (Romans 10:17). We hear His truth, believe His truth, and then see His truth manifest within our lives.

This was the example set by Abraham. He was "*fully persuaded that God had power to do what He had promised*" (Romans 4:21). His mind was made up concerning what he had heard God say. The world would have called him foolish for believing a one-hundred-year-old man could father a son with a ninety-year-old woman. Against hope he trusted that God's truth was greater than his facts. He was fully persuaded.

Being receptive to God's word requires a made-up mind. The more a mind is made up upon His truth, the more fruit that mind will manifest.

Walking In Wisdom

I count it an extreme honor to have stood alongside Steve as he faced his greatest battle. His walk during that season was a message that shouted more than words ever could. Those close to him heard it loud and clear. You never know what a person is truly made of until you see them face the fires of adversity. Through that fire he shined like gold.

Steve once said that "a soldier is not tested in the barracks, they are tested on the battlefield." That's exactly where he lived his life—on the battlefield fighting Hell for the lost souls of men. He said we were watching him fight *through* the greatest trial of his life. "I'm going through this," Steve would say. "I'm coming out the other side."

That was Steve, always the optimist in every situation. He processed everything through the lens of eternity. There were times the pain of the cancer would be so intense that he couldn't hold it in anymore. He would cry out in agony. You felt helpless—there was nothing you could do except be at his side. He would then compose himself and ask that we not be concerned about his pain. "This is nothing compared to the suffering our Savior endured on the cross," he would say. "Oh the pain, no one could imagine that sort of pain."

I miss the times we spent together sitting in his office as he spoke of the things he learned in the past and then we would dream of the future. He shared much wisdom during those times and I'm eternally grateful for those moments, but the most impactful thing for me was not found in what he said, but in what I saw.

For ten years I was able to see another side of the man of God. The one that lives away from the platform. I saw the kind of faithful father he was to his children, the devoted husband he was to his wife, and the kind of person he was when few were looking. As impressive as he was behind a pulpit, I was even more impressed by who he was as a person.

Steve showed what a life of complete trust looked like. His mind was made up on the things of Christ. His faith was in Jesus alone. The Christian faith is just that: faith. It's a relationship of trust and dependence upon Christ and His word. Steve trusted that everything taking place was for a reason and that God would get the glory.

He took comfort in Paul's words: "*For I consider that the sufferings of this present time are not worthy to be compared with the glory which shall be revealed in us.*" He never asked why. He didn't have to. He knew that "*all things work together for good to those who love God, to those who are the called according to His purpose*" (Romans 8:18, 28).

When Steve was raised up from his deathbed we all glimpsed a part of that glory. I stood with Steve on a stage as he preached his first message after his brush with death. Thousands filled the auditorium and millions watched on TV. As he spoke I couldn't help but think that just one year earlier doctors had said this moment I was witnessing was impossible. The Lord had answered Steve's prayer!

My friend, you can make up your mind upon God's word and live life according to that truth. Learning to trust God and His word in every situation is the only work Jesus burdened us with. He said, "*This is the work of God, that you believe in Him whom He sent*" (John 6:29). Simply believe!

Solomon wrote, "*Trust in the Lord with all your heart, and do not lean on your own understanding. In all your ways acknowledge Him, and He will make straight your paths*" (Proverbs 3:5-6).

God's ways are not our ways. His perspective is perfect and therefore His path is as well. When we trust what we know we limit ourselves to what we can see, but when we trust what He knows we are lifted to what He sees. This is the key to finding success in anything you will attempt to do.

Materially speaking Solomon was a very successful king. He achieved more and amassed more in the natural not because he trusted his understanding but God's. Solomon didn't trust what he knew, he trusted what God knew. In the secret place of prayer he asked to know God's wisdom (2 Chronicles 1:10).

A. W. Tozer writes this about wisdom, "Wisdom…is the ability to devise perfect ends and to achieve those ends by the most perfect means. It sees the end from the beginning, so there can be no need to guess or conjecture. Wisdom sees everything in focus, each in proper relation to all, and is thus able to work toward predestined goals with flawless precision."[1]

Wisdom is the ways of God. It is the application of God's truth to any situation and circumstance we face. It is approaching our problems and opportunities the way God would and getting God's results. Can you imagine the possibilities?

What if you knew that every decision you would make today was the absolute right decision? Imagine you approach today without a single doubt or fear. You have no uncertainty regarding your choices. Every decision concerning what to do, where to go, what to say, and how to invest is perfect. If that were true, what would be impossible for you? Nothing!

Anything and everything you desired or endeavored to do would suddenly open up to you. You would find all things to be possible. Sound familiar? *"If you can believe, all things are possible to him who believes"* (Mark 9:23).

This is the power of a mind made up upon God's truth; not just any truth, God's truth. A mind that is set upon a lie can only expect the fruit of that lie to manifest. Make up your mind upon His truth and suddenly all things become possible. Not some things, all things! The infinite possibilities of God become possible to those who fully believe His truth.

Steve also showed what a life of prayer looked like. If you really want to know what a man is like you need only spend an hour in prayer with him. A man can wear a disguise in public whether he is on the street or the sanctuary but in the private place of prayer you are stripped bare. Steve was a man of deep devotion who sought to live his life close to God's throne with his ears open to the still-small whispers of the Lord.

This is the chamber in which receptivity is cultivated. The knowledge of God's wisdom and ways can only come from spending time with Him. Jesus said it "*has been given to you to know the mysteries of the kingdom of heaven*" (Matthew 13:11). Paul writes this concerning these mysteries: *"We speak wisdom among those who are mature, yet not the wisdom of this age, nor of the rulers of this age, who are coming to nothing. But we speak the wisdom of God in a mystery, the hidden wisdom which God ordained before the ages for our glory"* (1 Corinthians 2:6-7). This wisdom is stored up for those willing to come humbly before Him with clean hands and pure hearts.

This is the exact place He taught His disciples to go. Consider again the disciples' encounter with the demon-possessed boy. After failing to bring about deliverance, the disciples ask the cause. In the spiritual world failure can only have one cause: a lack of faith. Jesus said it is *"because of your unbelief"* (Matthew 17:20). Then, after diagnosing the problem, Jesus offers the solution: *"This kind comes out only by much prayer and fasting"* (Matthew 17:21).

The prayer and fasting Jesus was calling for was not about the spirit in the boy, but about the spirit in the disciples. Jesus revealed to them how their lack of prayer was producing a lack of power within their lives. The disciples were not men of much faith, because they were not men of much prayer. The more time we spend in His face, the more it builds our faith. Had the disciples been men of much prayer they would have been men of much presence. They would have known God and His ways and been able to manifest His power when the time called for it.

Andrew Murray, a classic Christian writer and missionary to South Africa, wrote, "Faith can only live by feeding on what is divine, on God Himself." We feed upon God in that place of prayer and fasting. Murray continues, "Prayer is the one hand with which we grasp the invisible; fasting, the other, with which we let loose and cast away the visible."[2] Through prayer we take hold of His kingdom, and through fasting we let go of ours.

Time with the Lord teaches us to become more receptive to His voice. Times of fasting allow us to become less receptive to all other voices.

Steve showed the rewards of a receptive life. Steve led the longest-running revival in American history, won millions of souls for the kingdom and did more in his short thirty years of ministry than many could hope to do in a lifetime.

As believers we are called to do great exploits for the Lord. D.L. Moody once said, "If God be your partner, make your plans large." God doesn't think small. Everything He does is great. Seeing God's success in any and every situation is the reward of those who live with their ears turned toward His wisdom.

It does not matter if you are in full-time ministry, a businessman, a parent, or an employee, there is a reward to be found in being receptive. Every one of us desires to be successful in all our endeavors. There is a guaranteed way to find God's success.

Make up your mind concerning His truth and seek to apply it toward this day. Andrew Murray, still writing about faith, says, "It is the simplest, so it is the highest exercise of the spiritual life, where our spirit yields itself in perfect receptivity to God's Spirit and so is strengthened to its highest activity. This faith depends entirely upon the state of the spiritual life; only when this is strong and in full health, when the Spirit of God has full sway in our life, is there the power of faith to do its mighty deeds."[3]

The most damaging individual to the enemy is a person with a made-up mind. Such a man or woman is unflinching in adversity and unstoppable in their faith. They see obstacles as opportunities and trust that if God be for them, who can be against them (Romans 8:31). They step into their day with fully persuaded minds and agitate the complacent and frustrate their foes.

There is a reward for walking in God's ways. The path is already blessed. Regardless of the situation you face at this moment, you can turn your ears toward His wisdom and apply it. James writes, "*If any of you lacks wisdom, let him ask of God, who gives to all liberally and without reproach, and it will be given to him. But let him ask in faith, with no doubting*" (James 1:5-6).

Those who live with their ears turned to Heaven need only ask and God will speak. When He speaks, don't doubt; just obey. Faith for the believer is spelled obedience. Therefore, walk out His words in obedience and don't doubt! You can trust that God's wisdom brings certainty to your steps and His ways guarantee His results.

> *Lord, show me Your ways and teach me Your wisdom. I desire to find that place in You where my ears are attentive to Your voice and my mind is made up concerning Your truth. Bless the work of my hands and order my footsteps.*

NOTES

1. A. W. Tozer, *The Knowledge of the Holy* (New York, NY: HarperCollins, 1961), 60.
2. Andrew Murray, *The Prayer Life* (Amazon Digital Services, Inc., 2010), Kindle location 2379.
3. Ibid., Kindle location 2368.

Chapter Eight

Heed How You Hear

Not just what you hear, but how you hear

"Therefore take heed how you hear."
—Luke 8:18, NIV

We had a vintage Curtis Mathes radio that once belonged to my grandparents. They bought it new in the '60s to be the centerpiece of their living room. My father remembers lying on the floor as a teenager listening to the first Frazier vs. Ali fight on that radio. That was before my time, but I'm certainly jealous of the memory.

The radio was not small. It was the size of a long dresser and made out of solid panels of dark walnut. It was a beautiful cabinet that looked more like it was purchased at a furniture retailer than an electronics store. It had two large stereo speakers neatly concealed on the right and left behind grill cloth and wood slats. The radio was cleverly hidden underneath the top of the console. Getting to it was simple—you just had to raise the lid.

Unlike most modern units, this system was not hard to operate. There was one button to turn it on or off, a switch for picking AM or FM, and then four rotating knobs positioned just below the dial face. Three knobs were for controlling the volume, balance, and tone. The fourth was for tuning. That's it. It was state-of-the-art technology at the time. Now it's just a beautiful memory of a bygone era.

Of course it couldn't compete with the crisp and clear surround sound of my current A/V receiver. However, I don't treasure the new system the way I do that old Curtis Mathes. I think about that antique radio, remembering the static and white noise that would hiss, crack, and pop alongside the music and the distinct smell of the transistors heating the dust that collected on its coils. I'm taken back to a simpler time. A time when families would gather in the living room to just listen.

Today there is so much vying for our attention that the art of slowing down and listening is lost to us. I long for those times of sitting comfortably in the silence of a moment listening to a single source. We lose so much because we can't concentrate. We expect and anticipate to be entertained with a constant barrage of stimuli coming from multiple sources and all at once. It's a chaotic mess that makes truly hearing any one thing an impossibility.

Some may consider this nostalgic longing for the sweet simplicity of sitting still to be a mundane use of time. My friend, with everything we are watching and listening to, we don't know how much we're actually missing. Until we learn to listen, we have little hope of becoming receptive to the one voice we so desperately need to hear.

Even now that voice is speaking. Just as He spoke to His disciples, He is speaking to us: *"Take heed **how** you hear."* Not just *what* you hear, but *how* you hear as well. If you are listening to the Lord, then you can trust the *what.* He is the one responsible for that, and His word is faithful. The *how* is our responsibility.

ARE YOU LISTENING?

When I was a child there wasn't a lot of choices of what to listen to on that old radio. There were two Christian stations in the area. One played preaching all day, the other played music. You could have your own church service any time, just by switching between the two.

We had a local AM station whose highlight of the morning was called the "Flea Market Show." Listeners would call in to share an item they had up for sale. One caller would offer up an old car; the next would be selling a pig. Yes, that says a lot about the region I grew up in. Believe it or not, this was the most popular show in town. Alongside these three we had a handful of rock, classic, and country stations. In total, there were a dozen choices.

Finding the station you wanted to listen to was a matter of turning the dial. I mention this for those who are unfamiliar with an old analog radio. Finding a station wasn't as easy as pushing a button. You had to dial it in. Turning the tuning knob would move a needle across the printed dial face that was numbered from 88 to 108. As the needle moved up the dial you'd hear the static change its tone. When you neared a radio station, the sound of music or talking would start to break through the white noise. Dialing in the station required a little finesse. A slight twist too far and the signal would be lost.

Those numbers correspond to a radio frequency. Each station has its own unique frequency that it broadcasts at. Turning the dial of the radio sets the device to receive that particular frequency. At any time during the day, dozens of radio signals were available to be listened to. They quietly filled the air just waiting for someone to tune in.

Jenna and I were ministering to a couple that was going through a difficult season. The husband had been out of work for some time. Their bank account was deep in the red. This pressure was multiplied by the fact they were caring for two additional members of their extended family. Both felt they couldn't hang on much longer. The wife made a comment in frustration that I've heard many times before expressed in many different ways. She said, "Through all this, I feel like I'm in a spiritual drought, it's been so long since I've heard God speak to me. I wish He would just say something to me."

She felt alone and believed God was purposely isolating her by His silence. Perhaps you can relate. You may feel as if you are sitting waiting for God to speak. Listen, though you may be surrounded by silence, God Himself is never silent. He doesn't withhold His voice from us. He is speaking, we just have to tune in and listen.

Jesus showed us what a receptive life looks like. He enjoyed unbroken communication with His Father. He was sustained through His trials and tests by His Father's word. He had never known silence until He hung upon the cross. There He took upon himself our sin and that line of communication was broken for the first and only time. Jesus cried out, *"My Father, my Father why have you forsaken me"* (Luke 8:8). He was now alone hanging between Heaven and earth.

Because of that moment, you and I will never have to pray that prayer. Jesus was forsaken so that we will never be forsaken. He promised to never leave us or forsake us. Just as manna was provided daily for the Israelites in the desert, you can expect that His word is waiting fresh and new for you each day as well. However, unlike that manna, which perished with the day, the bread that Christ offers is imperishable and superior in every way.

If you are sitting in silence or find listening to His voice difficult through all the noise, it's time to adjust the dial and tune in to the voice that has been speaking all along.

ARE YOU UNDERSTANDING?

Jesus concludes the parable with an exclamation: "He who has ears to hear, let him hear!" Everyone gathered that day heard the parable, but very few understood it. The crowd wasn't dialed in, but the disciples were beginning to. They wanted to know more.

The word *parable* means "to cast alongside." A parable is an analogy that is "cast alongside" a principle to make the meaning clear. Jesus knew that the truths of the kingdom of God were foreign to the worldly thinking of man. So He painted kingdom truths into parables that we could easily understand. That is if we have ears to hear. Most would hear the parable and leave it at a simple story while those with receptive spirits would seek the greater truth hidden within.

Isn't it interesting that not only do you cast seed, but you also cast a parable? Do you see the parallel? Jesus uses this parable like seed and casts it upon the multitude. Within that crowd the seed found the four soils spoken about in the parable. They were all present that afternoon. The religious and hard-hearted immediately rejected it. They didn't want to hear what Jesus had to say. The shallow-hearted loved what they were hearing, but lost it as soon as they departed. The double-minded couldn't grasp it either. They were too caught up with their own worries to truly hear what He was saying. The disciples were the only ones to grab the parable and inquire more. They were beginning to let it settle within their hearts and started to inquire about it.

Having ears to hear means not just hearing the words—it means that we actually begin to think and meditate upon them. This is how we begin to hear God's word more clearly. When God speaks to us through His word, through the words of someone else, or by His still-small voice, we should take that seed and let it settle into the soil of our lives. The psalmist David said, "*I have hidden your word in my heart*" (Psalm 119:11). When a seed is hidden in the soil it begins the process of germination. The seed starts to transform and grow. Suddenly the truth contained within the word begins to open up and we realize there is so much more than just what we heard at first.

This is why I encourage believers to take time when reading scripture. It is too easy to get caught up in a reading plan that causes you to fly through chapters so you can check off your reading for the day. How can you truly receive from the word if you aren't taking the time to let it get into you? This is why Steve Hill would remind us often, "Don't just go through the book; let the book go through you!"

You would be far more productive to read one verse and meditate on it throughout the day than to read several chapters you can't recall. A Bible sitting on the shelf does you no good, but when it's hidden in your heart, it does a world of good.

Joshua said, "*This Book of the Law shall not depart from your mouth, but you shall meditate in it day and night, that you may observe to do according to all that is written in it. For then you will make your way prosperous, and then you will have good success*" (Joshua 1:8). Meditation is not a spiritual discipline most know how to exercise. It simply means to ponder and focus on a thought over and over again.

When God speaks, take the time to meditate upon it. Let that seed be driven deep within you and watch as it begins to open up. His words, like the air we breathe, are life to us. You don't just breathe once a day and consider that to be enough. You continually draw it in and out. Oxygen is continually on your lips as it fills your lungs, day and night. Similarly take that word and let it be drawn in and out of you. Think about it throughout the day. Take a moment and ponder each word He spoke. As you meditate you will begin to see His truth unfold.

Jesus said that this seed contained "*the mysteries of the kingdom of God*" (Luke 8:10). A "mystery" is a spiritual truth that can only be understood by divine revelation. He said that these "secrets" were reserved for those who were on the inside. The door to the inside is easy to find and open to those with ears to hear. These receptive individuals have chosen to come close to Jesus and learn from Him and obey Him. To them the secrets are assured to open up.

As Jesus explains the soils, He offers another parable to the disciples. He says, "*No one, when he has lit a lamp, covers it with a vessel or puts it under a bed, but sets it on a lampstand, that those who enter may see the light. For nothing is secret that will not be revealed, nor anything hidden that will not be known and come to light*" (Mark 4:16-17).

We live in the Information Age. It is a time when knowledge and technology are advancing by the day. We are discovering mysteries contained within the smallest of particles on earth as well as in the farthest reaches of the universe. All of this vast amount of human wisdom is freely and instantly made available at the touch a button. If there is something you want to know, you can learn without delay.

Our lives are filled with a variety of devices for consuming all kinds of content, be it music, video, voice, or text. We have instant access to more information and media than a person could ever consume in the whole of a life. The entire knowledge of humanity is waiting on you to simply download it.

All this information fills the air around you. Right now where you sit there is an incalculable amount of radio waves silently bombarding you from radio stations, television stations, cellular towers, and satellites, not to mention the hundreds of individual devices surrounding you that are all connected wirelessly to a network of some sort. These electromagnetic waves are filling the air all around you at this moment, but you can't see or hear any of them—that is, unless you have the right device that can receive one signal, then interrupt that signal in a way you can understand.

The arrival of Jesus marked the beginning of a kingdom information age. He said that the mysteries of the kingdom are now fully revealed. They shine forth like a light within a dark room. It's not hidden; it's in the open. Anyone with willing ears, who inquires of the Lord, can discover them at this moment.

We live in the greatest days of church history! The prophets of old saw visions of this day but did not get to be a participator. They longed for such an experience. They were jealous to have such access to the kingdom of God. Yet we take it for granted. The Lord has made His secrets available, yet for the most part we refuse to listen.

This is what Jesus told His disciples when He said, "*Blessed are your eyes for they see, and your ears for they hear; for assuredly, I say to you that many prophets and righteous men desired to see what you see, and did not see it, and to hear what you hear, and did not hear it*" (Matthew 13:16-17).

He has brought us to an ocean filled with His precious secrets—we take a cup, dip it into the waters, and are content with what we can hold within our grasp. What a shame when so much is waiting for you. Why not relinquish the cup and jump into the waters? Loose yourself from this noisy world and abandon yourself in the serene secret depths of His kingdom—that's the only way to truly hear.

The secrets of God's kingdom are hidden inside the seeds of His word. They contain the very words of life itself. Those willing to be lost in the depth of who He is will discover the mysteries contained within. What a time you and I live in and what access He has given to those who choose to hear. To let the seeds of His word sit within the soil of their heart and germinate to bring forth much fruit.

His truth is hidden in plain sight within His light. It's out in the open. It's the perfect hiding place because no one can say "you didn't tell me" or "I couldn't find it." It was there all along in the light that shines forth in the darkness. Those who are afraid of the light because it reveals everything about them run from the light and hide in the darkness. But those who step into the light find that not only does the light reveal us, it reveals Him as well.

Solomon wrote, "*It is the glory of God to conceal a matter but the glory of kings is to search out a matter*" (Proverbs 25:2). The Lord has secrets and He shares them, but only to those who have ears to hear. His glory is found concealed within the light of His word. They are precious treasures waiting to be mined by those willing to search them out. Paul echoes, "*For it is God who commanded light to shine out of darkness, who has shone in our hearts to give the light of the knowledge of the glory of God in the face of Jesus Christ*" (2 Corinthians 4:6).

Truly in Christ is light and that light is our life. It shines forth in the darkness and those who choose to step into and live in the light find a kingdom they knew not of. The light is His glory. It is cultivated by spending time staring into the face of Jesus and coming to truly know Him. Not merely through the stories we hear about Him, but through a genuine encounter with His presence.

HOW ARE YOU LISTENING?

Jesus has shared the parable with the multitudes. The disciples have come in private to ponder the deeper meaning behind Christ's words. He has revealed to them that the secret mysteries of His wisdom are now fully available to those who have ears to hear. Now He commands them, "*Therefore take heed how you hear*" (Luke 8:18). This is the key to receptivity.

Jesus, with great patience and generosity, has done His part—now He says the responsibility rests upon the hearers. It is the hearer who determines how receptive they will be. He makes it clear: you have the ability to cultivate the soil of your life to how receptive you will be to His word. You are the one who determines what kind of soil you will be. Will you be hard-hearted, shallow-hearted, or double-minded, or will you be receptive? You make the decision how you hear.

PRESENT HARVEST IS PREVIOUS SEED

Consider your life at this moment. Everything that you have or don't have. Everything that you know. Everything that you are going through is the direct result of decisions you've made in the past. You are reaping a present harvest of the seeds you've previously sown.

The word of God says that as long as the earth remains there will be seed time and harvest. It also says that as a man sows, so shall he reap. Unfortunately, we tend to think of sowing and reaping solely in terms of giving. Nevertheless, the principle of sowing and reaping applies to every aspect of life. It's the system God established upon the earth and it will endure as long as the earth remains.

You have to understand that everything about your life right now is the fruit of seeds that have been sown in the past. Take every decision you've ever made—the good decisions, the bad ones, even the indifferent ones—add them all up, and the sum total of those decisions equals who you are at this moment. Present harvest is previous seed.

Want to know how well you are hearing God's word? Are you curious how receptive you are? Just look at your present harvest. What I see in my life is the result of how well I'm hearing His voice.

Jesus promised that those who were attentive to His word and considered carefully how they heard would reap an incredible harvest from that word. "*Therefore take heed how you hear. For whoever has, to him more will be given; and whoever does not have, even what he seems to have will be taken from him*" (Luke 8:18-19).

Jesus even went so far as to say that some would receive thirty, sixty, and even one hundredfold in return. The more receptive I am to His word and voice the greater I can expect His word to multiply within me producing a greater harvest in return. Good seed *plus* good soil *equals* a great harvest. This simple equation says it well.

His seed is good. It never returns to Him void. I can trust the seed. So the only thing I need to work on is the soil and I have the ability to cultivate that to be receptive to Him.

Here is the great news: if I don't like the present harvest I see in my life, I can change it by sowing differently now. No sense continuing to do things the same way you always have expecting it to magically produce a different outcome in the future. I can change it if I change my soil!

Get this and you are at the initiation point of a completely different and more fulfilling relationship with the Lord. One full of the abundant life He promised.

As I write this I hear my stereo in the background. We like to keep worship music playing throughout our home as it helps create an atmosphere of peace. Because it is always on, it is easy to hear the music but not pay it attention. I've grown accustomed to it and take it for granted.

It is hard to imagine that we could take Christ's words for granted, but we do. Today's believer has access to more teaching and resources then any scholar who has ever lived. We can listen to the greatest teachers and access the libraries of the greatest theologians any time we want and wherever we want. However, with all that is available, we still walk so immaturely. Why? It's all background noise.

SO MUCH TRUTH, SO LITTLE FRUIT

Even the voice of our Savior is ignored. He speaks, we barely listen. He continues to speak, we continue to turn deaf ears. He offers His words and we contend that He is silent. My friends, He is doing His part—we are not. Our fruit rests on us changing this.

Jesus makes it clear that we have the ability to control how receptive we are to His voice. We are the ones who will determine whether or not we see a thirty, sixty, or one hundredfold return on His truth within our life—the key is: How are you listening?

Take a look at the fruit on your tree. Are you walking in the promises and provisions of the Lord? Is His wisdom marking your life? How is your walk and relationship with the Lord? If you don't like the fruit you see, don't get discouraged—get receptive.

I mentioned that old radio takes me back, though not to my childhood. It is a connection to a different time that I didn't grow up in—I've only heard about it in the stories of those who lived it. It was a simpler time with a people who had a simpler faith. They certainly didn't have all that we have, but we've lost something they had.

I was sitting with Pop, the last year of his life. He was reminiscing about a revival they saw take place during the 1950s at an old tobacco barn that had been converted to a meeting hall. He said you walked in and would see the ceiling covered with suspended wheelchairs, canes, walkers, slings, and other items. These trophies silently testified of the miracles that had just taken place. He said, "Daniel it was impossible not to get someone healed in those days. You had faith for anything." Then with tears in his eyes he asked, "What happened?"

What happened isn't that God changed—we did. These precious saints knew what it was to wait upon the Lord. They would tarry through the night if need be to pray through to a victory. They had a faith that depended upon hearing His word. They knew how to sit and listen.

Today we are lost in the busyness of our lives. There is so much noise. So much clamoring for our attention that finding a place to simply sit and listen to His voice is difficult. With all that we have available, we see so little.

It's time to learn a lesson from that old radio. It's past time to get back to a place where we can truly hear His voice and let it penetrate deep into our hearts. It's time to take heed how we hear. He is doing His part, now it's our turn to do ours.

> *Lord, help me to take heed how I hear You. I understand I am the one who determines how receptive I am to Your voice. Give me the wisdom to tune in to Your gentle whispers. Help me to find that quiet place where I can still myself and simply listen to You.*

Chapter Nine

The Constant Speaking Voice of God

God is always speaking—are you always listening?

"Man shall not live by bread alone, but by every word that proceeds from the mouth of God."
—MATTHEW 4:4

How did I miss it? It was there in front of me the whole time but I just didn't see it. This was my first lesson in the art of communication with my wife and one that I failed miserably.

Jenna and I were newlyweds. We had only been married a month when we moved from South Carolina to Texas to begin the adventure of church planting in the Dallas/Fort Worth metroplex. Yes, we were starting a family and a church at the same time. Some may think that is a bit much to tackle all at once. Not us—we've always thrived in changing environments.

We had moved into a little apartment close by the church and were getting settled into our new life together. All the boxes were unloaded and our new home was all set up. We didn't have much, but it was enough to make it feel like home. Our friends and family had blessed us with some wonderful gifts for our wedding. There was one in particular that we were especially excited to try. It was an espresso machine.

Jenna and I are both coffee lovers. We enjoy starting our mornings together sitting in the living room talking over a fresh cup of coffee. It's a daily date that we try our best not to miss. I could blame that little espresso machine for our obsession.

It had been a few weeks and I had gotten to be pretty good at making cappuccinos and lattes with our little machine. It was certainly cheaper to make them at home than to spend ten times more at the corner coffee shop. One morning I got up before Jenna and made it to the kitchen before she did. I went straight to the machine. I found two coffee cups sitting in front of it. I thought it was strange that we had left cups sitting out, so I put one away and then steamed some milk to perfection, poured two shots, and made a decent cappuccino.

That's when it happened. Jenna came to the kitchen and looked at me with my cup in hand. She then got the most disappointed look on her face. Immediately I asked what was wrong.

She responded, "Why didn't you make me a cup?"

"I didn't know you wanted me to," I said.

Then she added, "That's why I left my *favorite cup* out for you to see."

How was I supposed to know that a cup on the counter was a request for coffee? Had she asked me, I would have gladly made one. In her mind she had asked and done so clearly. Her hardheaded husband just wasn't listening.

I didn't realize it at the time but she was setting me up. Typically she was the one who would get up early and make us both coffee. This morning she had put all the pieces in play for me to be the one who would bless her. She could have asked directly, and I would have gladly obliged. That's not what she wanted. I've learned that Jenna's primary "love languages" are gifts and acts of service. When someone selflessly does something for her or gives her a heartfelt gift it makes her feel loved. This morning a cup of coffee offered up by her husband would have been shouting "I love you" in both of those languages. She left the obvious bread crumbs trusting her loving spouse would follow them. I didn't.

She was speaking, but I wasn't listening. I hadn't learned all her different languages yet. In fact, I thought I was serving her by cleaning up the mess she had left on the counter. I tried to explain it that way to her...it didn't work. I've since learned from my missed opportunity.

Communication is so much more than words. There are many ways to say something. I can tell my wife I love her with my words or with my actions. A cup of coffee sometimes says it louder than the phrase. If we know how to hear and speak to one another our relationships are strengthened. This is true for any relationship, especially our one with the Lord.

God speaks in many different ways and is always speaking. He first spoke in the beginning—*"Let there be light"* (Genesis 1:3)—and has not been silent since. Just as the light that first shone through the darkness has never stopped, His voice has never been silenced. This is the constant speaking voice of God and those with discerning ears know how to tune in and listen. As mentioned before, I don't believe that God ever subjects us to silence. He may change the way He speaks, but He doesn't leave us to wander without the guiding light of His voice.

A. W. Tozer writes about this in *The Pursuit of God.* He says, "God is forever seeking to speak Himself out to His creation. The whole Bible supports the idea. God is speaking. Not God spoke, but God is speaking. He is by His nature continuously articulate. He fills the world with His speaking voice."[1]

Jesus lived within this place of constant communion with the Father. He said, "I only say what I hear the Father saying." That which He heard is what He spoke. The disciples hungered to know God in such a way. Seeing the intimacy of Jesus's relationship, they said, *"Lord, teach us to pray"* (Luke 11:1). He didn't deny them access to that secret place—he opened the door to it! There Jesus showed the potential relationship we too can enjoy. The door is now wide open and you can boldly step into the throne room and enjoy this communion with the Lord.

Jesus had known this constant communion with the Lord from the very beginning. There was never a time that stream of communication was broken. Not until the cross. There Jesus suffered the silence of the Lord, so that we would sit in silence no longer. That day on the cross the lines of communication were forever opened. Anyone who calls upon the name of the Lord now has access to the Father. You can step into that constant stream of His voice and hear Him. God is speaking—are you listening?

FIVE WAYS GOD SPEAKS

The most asked question I receive from both saints and sinners is, "How can I hear God's voice?" There is an innate desire within each of us to reach out and connect with our Creator and there is a deep sense that it must be possible. Hearing the voice of our Father is the most important spiritual discipline we can know. When we learn to hear His voice everything else finds its answer.

There is no how-to guide for hearing God's voice given in scripture. Anyone who would attempt to offer one is misleading you. The young prophet Samuel was merely a boy in the temple when he first heard the Lord calling. He mistook it for the voice of his elder prophet Eli. Samuel learned over time and interaction to recognize and hear the voice of the Lord. It is no different for us. God speaks and we mistake His voice. Thankfully He continues to call out to us. The more we interact with Him in relationship the more we become attuned to His unmistakable voice.

God speaks in different ways to different people. He called to Moses from fire. He spoke to Joseph through dreams. Elijah heard His still-small voice. David discerned His voice through creation. Jehoshaphat would inquire of the Lord through prophets. God spoke to the crowds from the clouds when Jesus was baptized. The Holy Spirit speaks through believers by words of knowledge, revelation, prophesy, and tongues. God speaks through visions. Most importantly He speaks through His word. The Lord can and will communicate through any of these and more.

Communication with the Lord is something that we learn through relationship. Jesus said, *"My sheep know my voice"* (John 10:27). He calls us His own. Those who are His come to know His voice over time.

When my children were born we learned to communicate with them in different ways as they grew. They didn't come out of the womb with a vast vocabulary. In fact, they only knew one sound and they exercised that until we figured out what they were saying to us.

I promise the moment you came into the Lord's kingdom your ears opened up and you began to hear. Like a child that learns over time, you too can learn to hear the voice of your Creator. If you have ears to hear, He will speak.

There are many ways the Lord will speak to us. All of them can all be grouped into five different categories. God will speak through what we feel and what we see. He uses others to speak to us. He speaks through His word and His still-small voice.

Feelings

This is the language we are most familiar with. Our feelings are powerful for arousing our attention and causing us to connect with another person. Great communicators look for a way to cause their listeners to identify emotionally with what they are saying. They know that emotional attachment causes greater receptivity. Truly there is no greater communicator than our Lord and He certainly knows how to touch our emotions to get our attention.

When so many have turned deaf ears to His word, emotion is often the only way we will listen. The backslidden sinner who finds himself in church knows this voice. As the preacher calls out his sin, encourages him to repent, and tells of God's grace, the man feels guilt. Godly conviction comes over him. His heart races; his palms begin to sweat. He knows that he must do something. He rushes to the altar and calls upon the Lord. He repents of his sins and confesses Jesus as Lord. Suddenly the guilt and conviction leaves and he is overwhelmed with peace. He doesn't realize it yet but he's already started to hear and respond to the voice of Lord.

There are times God will use our feelings to alert us to the immediate dangers around us. One night I was startled from a deep sleep. I had a sense something was wrong. Rather than ignore the feeling, I got up and looked out the bedroom window. Our back deck had just caught on fire. It was ignited from an ember that fell from a grill I had used hours earlier. Because I was attentive to this voice, I was able to extinguish the flames before any damage was done to our home.

Other times God uses our feelings to alert us to future problems. Perhaps you are working on a business deal, or you've been asked to do something that is unethical. You might be praying about a big decision you have to make. You don't feel peace when you think about it. Don't dismiss your feelings. That feeling is likely your spirit communicating that something is off. It is wise to probe deeper when these feelings come. What is causing concern? What is the Lord wanting to say?

Our feelings are a powerful way to communicate, but they are also prone to be misunderstood and can even be misleading. The Lord isn't the only one who will use our feelings to get our attention. The enemy and even some self-seeking individuals are skilled at manipulating emotions. This is why it is important to listen to your emotions, but not be led by them.

Feelings are fickle. Jesus wasn't led by what He felt, but what He saw and heard. It is possible you are standing in the right place, yet feel no peace. It could be you are in the wrong, yet feel right. Feelings alone offer no sure footing. Those who are led by their feelings will eventually be misled. You must stand on something more than just a feeling.

Signs

God not only speaks through our emotions, He uses signs as well. These signs can be dreams, visions, physical signs, situations, or circumstances. These are the things we see in the natural and spirit. They are signs that confirm and point toward what God is saying.

There is a great example of this in scripture found in the life of Joseph. He was a dreamer. The Lord spoke to him through two powerful dreams that showed him one day he would be given a position of leadership over his family. Joseph's older brothers despised his dreams and threw him into a ditch and sold him off into slavery. It seemed from the start those dreams would be aborted, but God's word is certain!

The situations that surrounded Joseph continued to get worse. He went from slavery to imprisonment. Nothing was going according to the dream. Then, after many years Joseph was miraculously brought out of prison to Pharaoh's palace. The previous slave and prisoner became a governor for all of Egypt.

Joseph's perspective shifted at the palace. He could now see how God used the situations and circumstances to bring him into the Lord's promises. He couldn't see it or hear it when he was a slave, but now everything he endured was shouting loud and clear. He was exactly where he was supposed to be. The dream was fulfilled.

Joseph's life became a powerful sign that spoke not only to Joseph and his family but still speaks to us today. All could clearly see God's plan and purposes at work. Joseph told his brothers, *"you meant evil against me; but God meant it for good"* (Gen 50:20). His story is a testament to how God will use signs and circumstances to confirm and accomplish His word.

God will open and close doors around us to position us within His promises. If you love the Lord and seek to live righteously you can trust that everything that surrounds you is taking you into the very things He has spoken. Some may be painful, others pleasant, but you can trust both are playing an important role in producing God's plan.

Pay attention to the signs around you. God can and will provide a sign to confirm His word but the signs themselves are not meant to communicate the specifics of His word. They point to it. Faith comes by hearing, not seeing. Many come looking for a sign, putting their faith in what they can see with their eyes, but faith comes by hearing. When we see a sign, we must inquire of the Lord, "What does this mean?"

We must also be careful here as well. We open ourselves up for deception when we allow ourselves to be led by the things we see. Just as Satan can manipulate our emotions, he is also capable of offering up his own signs. An example of this is found in the third and final temptation of Jesus. Satan brought Jesus to the top of a mountain and displayed before Him all the kingdoms of this world. This was a dramatic sign. Not only was it visually powerful but it also could be seen as the fulfillment of a divine promise. The Lord had spoken to His son, *"Ask of Me, and I will give You the nations for Your inheritance"* (Psalm 2:8). Satan now parades the nations, Jesus's inheritance, before Him and offers them if He will just bow down and worship.

Satan deceives many with this trick. He takes the promises of God and offers them up to us on a silver platter. The foolish take the bait without realizing it is from a deceptive source. Every open door and incredible opportunity is not God. Satan offered Jesus the world, but taking the bait would have caused Jesus to abandon the promise. Satan would love to cause you to do the same.

Thankfully, there is a reliable way to discern the signs we see. Jesus said, "*Away with you, Satan! For it is written, 'You shall worship the Lord your God, and Him only you shall serve*'" (Matthew 4:10). Satan's vision didn't line up with God's written word. The sign was false because it was not in harmony with what God spoke.

Remember: Jesus was led by what He saw and heard the Father say. The two always work in unison with one another. The signs point to the word and the word is confirmed by the signs that follow.

Others

God also speaks though the voice of others. He uses pastors, prophets, parents, and peers. Anyone can be a conduit for God's voice and discerning ears know how to listen.

When you gather together with the believers at your church to celebrate, expect God to speak throughout the service. If you are in the house He has called you to, then trust that God is using those in authority to communicate His word—don't dismiss it as "that doesn't apply to me." Listen for what does apply. The person who leaves their church saying that they "didn't get fed" doesn't know how to listen.

Paul says when we gather we should expect everyone to come with something from the Lord (1 Corinthians 14:26). These words are for the edification and building up of the body. I cherish the words of encouragement I receive from my peers who attend church with me. It may be delivered to the body or offered up individually in personal conversations. Listen for God's voice through those you worship alongside.

The Bible teaches, "*There is wisdom in the multitude of counselors*" (Proverbs 11:14). God uses those in authority to lead and guide us through life's difficult decisions. I am thankful I don't have to face those challenges alone—I can call upon the leaders and elders over me to help offer wisdom. God communicates through authority and the wise seek that counsel.

Some foolishly dismiss this. They contend that no man is without error, so they distrust the voice of authority. I understand no man is perfect, including this man. That is why I look for the safety found in many voices of wisdom. You can trust that if God establishes authority, He will also speak through it and honor those who listen.

The Word

Feel like you are experiencing a drought in your spiritual walk? Do you need to hear a word from the Lord? My friend you need only run to the written word. God's holy Bible is the clearest and most reliable communication from God. You can turn to any page in the word and within a few verses be caught up in hearing not only what He said, but also what He is saying. There is not another book like His book.

The written word is the captured word of God. It is what He spoke, and through those words He continues to speak. God allowed man to take paper and ink and place it within His constant speaking voice. Man then brought down to earth those pages divinely imprinted with His voice. The written word is the visible expression of His speaking voice.

Anything God says whether He uses our feelings, signs, circumstances, others, or even what we hear Him say within our spirit will align itself with His written word. It is the foundation upon which everything must be judged.

I've heard it said that experts who have trained their eyes to spot counterfeit currency or even counterfeit works of art do not spend time studying counterfeits. They spend countless hours studying the original. They come to know every mark and detail so that when a counterfeit comes along they can spot it immediately.

If you want to recognize God's voice, become an expert in His word. Spend countless hours studying what He said. Get to know His written word and you'll come to hear His spoken word. You'll immediately discern those counterfeit words that come to mislead. Time in His word tunes your spiritual ears.

The Still-Small Voice

Last we come to the still-small voice. These are His audible whispers spoken within our spirit and sometimes to our natural ears. This is the voice of God that calls out to those positioned in the secret place. This is the voice He desires us to become attuned to and to find confidence in.

Jesus said, *"Man shall not live by bread alone, but by every word that proceeds from the mouth of God"* (Matthew 4:4). Notice that *proceeds* is present tense. This is not just what God has said, but also what He is saying.

When you find this place you have found what it means to truly be in Christ. This is the place where you live, move, and have your being. This is where you can say, "I do what I see Jesus doing and say what I hear Him saying." This is the place God desires for you.

Just as His word is the imprinted text of His speaking voice, your life is also the expression of your own unique interaction with His voice. His words contain the very words of life. His words are light and that light is your life. God desires for His voice to make an imprint upon us so that you become an expression of His voice to those around you.

Solomon wrote, *"Wisdom is the principal thing; Therefore get wisdom"* (Proverbs 4:7). Worldly knowledge is obtained by our interaction with information. We send our children to school in order for them to interact with worldly knowledge. We load their minds down with information as we champion the merits of excelling in academics. We teach them that their worth is decided by their education. We celebrate intellect, but God desires wisdom. Spiritual wisdom is obtained by our interaction with God's written and spoken word. The secret place, that inner circle where God's mysteries and secrets are revealed to those with ears to hear, is where this takes place.

THE CHORUS OF VOICES

When He speaks you find that the chorus of these five voices are all in perfect harmony with one another. The feelings, the signs, the voices of authority, the written word, and the still-small voice will all be speaking the same thing. When you hear this unity within the voices you have confidence in what you are hearing.

Earlier I mentioned that Jenna and I transitioned to Texas to help plant a church. So much change happened in our lives during a single month. We got married, moved 972 miles from home, and started a new ministry. There was never a doubt in our minds that we were pursuing the voice and call of God for our lives.

There was plenty of excitement surrounding the move yet in the midst of all the change there was true peace and confidence. We knew it would be a challenge, but more importantly, we knew that God was with us.

In the natural the signs and circumstances were all pointing in this direction as well. We had both finished up school and the doors began to close in the ministry we were serving in. It was obvious we had come to the end of one season and this was the door that was opening to the next.

We were not the only ones who noticed this. We had the approval and recommendations of godly mentors. They all agreed that the Lord was in this next step and celebrated our transition. This was what both of us felt that we heard from the Lord and everything was in alignment with God's word. We had confidence we were hearing from the Lord.

We needed that. When the storms came and the trials and tests began to test the work we were endeavoring for in Texas, we could always rest that we were right in the middle of God's will. There were times when the stress of the moment would push us to the brink of throwing our hands up and walking away. I would ask Jenna if we were still called here and the answer was always a resounding, "Yes!"

Knowing what God spoke settled it. We could trust Him that no matter what came our way we would endure and emerge with victory.

Creating doubt in God's word is the challenge the enemy will always bring. He seeks to shake your confidence in what you heard because it is your connection to the kingdom. This is the secret to his crafty deceptions.

When Adam and Eve sinned in the garden it wasn't because Satan put the fruit before them and tempted them to eat. He was *"cunning"* as the scripture says. He challenged what they heard: *"Has God indeed said, 'You shall not eat of every tree of the garden?'"* (Genesis 3:1).

When you hear God speak, expect the voice of the enemy to immediately challenge it. "Did God really say that? Are you sure that wasn't your imagination? How can you be sure?" His tactic is to cause you to lose confidence in God's voice.

Eve responded to the devil. This was her first mistake. She should have commanded him to flee, but instead she engaged him in conversation. The moment we give place in our minds to a conversation with the enemy, we open the door to doubt and doubt creates double-mindedness. Eve says, "*We may eat the fruit of the trees of the garden; but of the fruit of the tree which is in the midst of the garden, God has said, 'You shall not eat it, nor shall you touch it, lest you die'*" (Genesis 3:2-3).

Notice Eve shared something extra that God never said. God had commanded them not to eat of the fruit, but nowhere does the scripture mention He said not to touch it. It is possible that Adam shared this extra word with his wife. Adam was the one who had heard the command from God and he brought that word to Eve. She likely had not heard it for herself. For Eve, the "how she heard" was diluted. God does use others to speak to us, but His desire is to speak to us directly. Had Eve enjoyed such a relationship with the Lord, perhaps she would not have been such easy prey for the devil.

The enemy saw the opportunity to pervert the word. This is why it is important to know what God said. You have to be in the word so that when the enemy speaks, you recognize the lies right away. The enemy is able to introduce doubt. I can see the snake wrapping himself around the tree, wrapping himself around the fruit, touching the fruit, and showing Eve that no harm has come to him. He then says, "*You will not surely die. For God knows that in the day you eat of it your eyes will be opened, and you will be like God, knowing good and evil*" (Genesis 3:5).

Faith comes by hearing and so does doubt. Because Eve was now listening to the wrong voice, doubt was introduced. Satan's trick worked and Eve took the bait.

Satan hasn't changed his mode of operation since. The next temptation we are privy to is Christ's temptation in the desert. This time the outcome is different.

Jesus has just been baptized and as He comes out of the water a voice from Heaven says, "*This is My beloved Son, in whom I am well pleased*" (Matthew 3:17). Immediately Jesus goes to the desert to be tempted by the devil.

Pay attention to how Satan begins: *"If you are the Son of God, command that these stones become bread"* (Matthew 4:3). What is Satan doing? This isn't about bread, it's about what was said. He heard the Father's word over Jesus, now he came to challenge it. "Did you really hear God say that? Do you really believe you are God's son? If you are then prove it! You're hungry, turn this stone to bread. Show me you are God's son." All three of Satan's temptations come as a direct challenge to God's word.

Jesus doesn't take the bait. He says, "*Man shall not live by bread alone, but by every word that proceeds from the mouth of God*" (Matthew 4:4). What word had just proceeded out of God's mouth? He had just heard God say, *"This is my son."* He didn't need to prove himself. He had a word from the Lord and that was enough.

When the enemy comes to shake your confidence in the voice of God learn from Christ. Don't engage him. When he spits out his lies, confess the word. You can place confidence in what is clearly written. You can hold fast to what God has said. The devil's arguments hold no ground against God's word. That word does not falter or fail.

The most important thing about you is your connection to God's constant speaking voice. Your ability to hear Him will lead you through the trials and tests of life into life in all its fullness. You can trust His voice and trust that He is not being silent. He is speaking at this very moment. He has been speaking all along. It's possible you haven't been truly listening. Look around you. There just might be a coffee cup sitting on the counter that you've missed.

Lord, You are always speaking; may I always listen! I cannot live by bread alone, but by the very words that proceed out of Your mouth. Help me to hear what You are saying. Teach me to hear Your voice through the many ways You speak.

NOTE

1. A. W. Tozer, *The Pursuit of God* (Harrisburg, PA: Christian Publications, 1948), 69.

Chapter Ten

Finding Your Secret Place

He who dwells in the secret place of the Most High
shall abide beneath the shadow of the Almighty.
PSALM 91:1

My favorite place of prayer is found in the corner of my home study. There is a window there that overlooks a park my children like to play in. Across the street between the homes you can see a wheat field that backs up to the neighborhood. I purposely positioned a comfortable recliner right by that window for this reason. Next to the chair sits an old wooden trunk that holds my study Bible and a beautiful leather-bound journal. This is my secret place.

The journal was a gift from Jenna that she gave me more than a decade ago. It was the week before the start of my final semester of Bible school. She had finished a semester earlier and now patiently and anxiously awaited my graduation. We were dating at the time and knew everything was about to change for us as this season was drawing to a close.

True to her nature, she took time finding a journal that fit my personality. It has a subtle brown cowhide leather cover. It looks rough from a distance, but is soft to the touch. I figure that's the way she likes to think of me. The edges are stitched with a lighter thread that gives it enough character to make it distinct while still maintaining a modest appearance. It's fitting for a man who longs for a humble place of prayer.

Throughout the journal you can find the marks of her thoughtfulness. She didn't just take this from a store shelf, wrap it up, and present it to me. Turning through the pages it is clear she spent time with it. Written in gold ink on the first page is a prayer she wrote specifically for me. It is obvious from the perfect flow of ink on the page that this was a prayer she had prayed many times before. She didn't have to think about it. She simply transcribed words from her heart. I'll find pages where she wrote her favorite scriptures concerning me as I've made my way through its pages. These little gems always warm my heart when I discover them. This is a gift that I've cherished to this day. She purposely sowed it into my own prayer life knowing that our relationship with each other could only be as strong as our relationship with our God.

You can look through that journal and learn a lot about my prayer life over the past thirteen years. The written pages contain precious truths the Lord has spoken to me over the years. The blank pages are still patiently waiting for the next truth I will discover. I don't write just anything, only the nuggets of gold the Lord speaks to me in the secret place. That book is my own personal treasure trove of God thoughts.

I was in prayer on August 8, 2012, when I got a notion to thumb through the journal. It had been some time since I had last done that. I picked up and glanced at the very first entry, which was dated August 8, 2002. It was ten years to the day. What I wrote a decade earlier had turned out to be truly prophetic for my life. Tears welled up in my eyes as I read the first verse of Psalm 91: *"He who dwells in the secret place of the Most High shall abide beneath the shadow of the Almighty."* Under that verse I wrote these words: May this be my life's prayer.

I couldn't have known then how much that verse would guide my life. More than a decade later, I find that everything for me has always come back to Psalm 91. It's my life message and it continues to be my greatest pursuit. I've sought out this secret place for thirteen years and feel I am just now beginning to understand what it means to dwell there. I pray an ember from my own secret place might spark something in you to seek yours out as well.

Leonard Ravenhill wrote, "No man is greater than his prayer life. The pastor who is not praying is playing; the people who are not praying are straying."[1] How true! A man who is weak in prayer is weak everywhere. No man can stand until he first learns to kneel. The road of the receptive spirit is one that is paved upon your knees. I know of no better place on earth to cultivate such a spirit than the secret place.

Everyone has their own secret place. It is the place you retreat to for times of rest and refuge. It is where you turn when life turns against you. Though it is different for each of us, we all have one. Some find refuge in their career—they try to lose themselves in their work. Some find that hiding place in their hobbies. They will tinker in a garage, a basement, or an attic with a project for hours hoping to escape the stress of the day. Others try to hide at the local bar seeking to bury their despair at the end of a bottle.

A secret place can be beneficial or detrimental. Choosing the right ones are imperative. When the world around you begins to shudder, or you feel as though you're sitting stagnant, you're likely to go running to your primary place of refuge. Like a compass that is shaken will always return to north, your heart will reach toward that familiar place of rest when you too are shaken. What is that place for you?

More than a decade ago I sought to make that place the secret place of the Lord. When my life is out of balance and things are turbulent, I come running to His shadow. Every morning I search it out knowing it's the only thing that orients me in the right direction and gives purpose to my day. I've become more and more obsessed with spending time there. The reward has been a richer walk with the Lord and ears tuned to His voice. My time has become more productive and my work more rewarding. I've become like a miner who has found a precious vein hidden within the deep recesses of a mountain. It is a treasure buried in a field that has cost everything, but nothing else compares. My friend that same treasure is patiently awaiting any who would choose the Lord's secret place.

Psalm 91 was not written by David, it was written by Moses. This is important to realize because Moses enjoyed a relationship with the Lord that we should all be jealous for. The Lord "*spoke to Moses face to face, as a man speaks to his friend*" (Exodus 33:11). Oh to know such intimate communion with the Lord! I like to think this psalm was lifted from Moses's own prayer journal so that we might get a glimpse into his own secret place and accept the invitation into our own.

I can imagine the setting. Moses is alone in a tent that he positioned outside the Israelite camp. He called it the *"tent of meeting."* Anyone who wanted to inquire of the Lord was welcome to come. Moses came inquiring often (Exodus 33:7).

The Israelites have been encamped in the desert wilderness of the Sinai Peninsula for eleven months. Moses has just returned from the summit of the mountain of God after having spent another forty days before the Lord. It was his eighth and final ascent up the mount. The encounter that took place there forever marked his life.

By the dim light of an oil lamp Moses takes a pen made from a hollow reed and fills it with ink. He had learned to make his own ink in Egypt from the sap and burnt charcoal of an acacia tree. His time and education in Egypt had provided him the tools and knowledge to preserve his thoughts for generations after. How blessed we are that he did. Strange to think how God used the captivity of Israel to also educate their leader to be the first one to record His word upon paper. Such as it is with the Lord. He is always at work for the good of those who love Him. Even in our trials and tests there is a purpose.

Fresh on the heels of his divine encounter, Moses lays the pen to a piece of papyrus and begins to scribe these words: "*He who dwells in the secret place.*" I wonder: Does Moses stop to consider the great diversity of dwelling places he has known in the past? Having grown up in the luxury of Pharaoh's palace, he has already tasted the very best man can offer; then, having been exiled from his birthplace, he came to know the humble dwelling of a Bedouin's tent. He has known both a life of living in excess and a life of living in lack. Now Moses writes of a dwelling place in which no other can compare.

A dwelling is your place of residence. It is where you have purposefully chosen to live your life. It's the home you build. Spiritually speaking, this is the relationship you are building with the Lord. Jesus said, "*Behold, I stand at the door and knock. If anyone hears My voice and opens the door, I will come in to him and dine with him, and he with Me*" (Revelation 3:20). The moment you said *yes* to Christ you came into a covenant relationship with Him. Much like a newlywed couple that leaves the homes of their parents to create a new dwelling place together, you have left the worldly home of your past behind to build a new dwelling place with the Lord. Take care to consider what kind of home that will be.

Moses chose to make his dwelling "*the secret place.*" This is a place that is hidden and obscure. It is only found by those who know where it is and have chosen to search it out. It is the exact place Jesus taught His disciples to go and pray. He said, "*When you pray, go into your room, and when you have shut your door, pray to your Father who is in the secret place; and your Father who sees in secret will reward you openly*" (Matthew 6:6).

Finding this place of obscurity is worth it. There is a reward awaiting those who choose to dwell there. Jesus called them the "*secrets and mysteries of the kingdom of God*" (Luke 8:10). Though it may be hidden, the door is always wide open to whosoever will enter. Pity so few ever do.

This wasn't any secret place—Moses wrote it was "*the secret place of the Most High.*" Did he pause when he wrote the name *Most High*? That word in Hebrew is *Elyon*. The Jewish people carry such reverence for the names of God. They do not use them in vain nor do they write them without showing great respect. *Elyon* translates to The Most High God. This is the name that communicates the reality of God's superiority over all things. He is the first and the last, the beginning and the end. Above Him there is no other, nor is there anyone like Him. He is truly the Most High. Our recognition of this truth is essential.

Moses, in the past, thought himself to be someone great having been raised as a prince of Egypt. Now he counted all those things as nothing compared to the all-surpassing worth of knowing the Most High God. He had come to the inescapable conclusion that he was nothing, while God was everything. Moses was content to live his life hidden in that reality.

The Lord is our all in all; without Him there is nothing at all. Living in and by this truth positions you within His greatness. This is where true humility is found and there is no greater hiding place than that. It is all about Him, and here I hide content to live my life in the obscurity of His majesty.

Moses takes his pen and refills it as he begins the second line. He is a gifted poet and his words are divinely inspired. He smiles as a tear wells up in his eye. His reed moves across the paper leaving in its wake the words "*shall abide beneath the shadow of the Almighty.*"

Take note that the first line, "*He who dwells in the secret place of the Most High*" is similar to the second, "*shall abide beneath the shadow of the Almighty.*" Hebrew poetry is different from Western poetry. We like to rhyme our words and structure the verses by the syllables. Hebrew poetry uses a lot of parallelism. The psalmist will often make a statement and then restate the same thought again using different words to better clarify their meaning. Every word in Hebrew carries significance and great care is taken to communicate it.

You can see the parallel of "*He who dwells*" in "*shall abide*"; "*in the secret place*" in "*beneath the shadow*"; and "*the Most High*" in "*the Almighty.*" Look for similar parallels next time you read a psalm. I guarantee that one little nugget will change the way you see them from then on.

The parallel of *dwelling* and *abiding* is an interesting choice. Your dwelling is the place where you have chosen to live your life. However, abiding means "to stay the night." One speaks of longevity over time, the other the brevity of a night. They are similar, but not the same. The two words together communicate an intimacy available in the place of constant communion, much like my wife and I are afforded the intimacy found in staying the night together in our own dwelling place.

This is where true rest and new life is found, abiding in His presence. When you choose to humble and hide yourself within the supremacy of who God is, you are invited to come into an intimate knowledge of who He is. We make the decision to enter into the dwelling place, now we are invited into a deeper relationship.

Moses writes that this abiding place of intimate rest is found "*in the shadow*." The secret place is the shadow of God. This phrase means "in the protection of." Just like a mother will throw herself in front of her children to protect them, the Lord places Himself before us. We are hidden in His shadow. My fights and struggles are now His, not mine. Victory does not rest on what I have within me, but upon what is found in Him. Moses parallels this thought in the second verse. He writes, "*I will say of the Lord, 'He is my refuge and my fortress.'*" The picture created with his words is of a cave or a mountain fortress. It is a place of safety and security hidden in the shadows of an impenetrable rock. There is no sweeter place to be found than hidden in the Lord's shadow. Tucked into the shadow of His rock.

Moses here calls this rock "*the Almighty*." This is the second name for God he uses. It is *el Shaddai* in Hebrew, which means "the all sufficient, all powerful, almighty God." It is a name the Israelites were well familiar with as it was the way God revealed himself to Abraham, Isaac, and Jacob. *El Shaddai* had proven time and time again that He would supply all their needs. He provided for Abraham in a land not his own. He provided an alternate sacrifice upon the mountain when Isaac was offered up. He opened the womb of Leah and Rachel to provide twelve sons for Jacob.

El Shaddai is our provider. Every good and perfect blessing comes from our Father who knows how to shower His children with everything we need. Moses shares that those who have positioned themselves and chosen to live their lives while hidden in the greatness of God are privileged to find a place of rest in the shadow of the one who provides everything they need. Every answer I seek can be found in Him. Every need can be met in Him. Anything is possible if I am living here in this secret place. Is this not powerful!

Many Hebrew scholars agree that *El Shaddai* might be expressed as "The Breasted One." As Scofield's Bible notes, "The etymological signification of Almighty God (El Shaddai) is both interesting and touching. God (El) signifies the "Strong One." The qualifying word *Shaddai* is formed from the Hebrew word *shad*, the breast...*Shaddai* therefore means primarily "the breasted."" The picture created is truly touching. A newborn knows what it is to find rest and nourishment in the shadow of his mother's breast. The child needs nothing else except their mom, just as you and I need nothing or no one else but our Almighty, all-sufficient God.

Moses paints a picture of a strong mountain fortress—a secret place hewn out in the midst of the rock. There you find a place of rest and receive the life-giving nourishment from the Lord. The Israelites knew the literal reality of this. Paul writes that Moses and the Israelites knew God in this way, for they "*all ate the same spiritual food, and all drank the same spiritual drink. For they drank of that spiritual Rock that followed them, and that Rock was Christ*" (1 Corinthians 10:3-4).

The shadow of that rock is where life-giving water springs forth. We literally drink from the rock! The secret place is found by those who make the rock their dwelling place, and that rock is Christ! Our secret place is found in no other place than in Christ Jesus, our Lord. For in Him we live and move and have our being (Acts 17:28). We can open the door of our lives to Him and allow Him to come in to make our lives a dwelling for Him. There in that place you discover the mysteries of truly knowing Him. He will hide us, shelter us, and protect us all while providing everything we need. For in Him we find "*everything we need pertaining to life and godliness*" (2 Peter 1:3).

This is God's desire for us and it always has been. He sent His Son to die upon that cruel cross so that we would be reconciled to Him and the door to this relationship would be opened up once again. Today that door stands wide open for whosoever would call on the name of Jesus. This is the invitation you see written from this page in Moses's own prayer journal.

The Bible says that when Moses would enter the tent of meeting that the people of Israel would all stand at the entrance of their own tents watching. The pillar of cloud and fire that led them through the desert would come move to the tent of meeting and there Moses would speak with God face-to-face. This was an extraordinary site to behold, but nothing could compare to what Moses saw within that secret place of meeting.

One of these encounters is recorded for us in Exodus 33. It is the background for Psalm 91. Moses had come to intercede on behalf of the people of Israel. The people had sinned against God by making a golden idol and worshiping it. All of this took place at the foot of Mount Sinai. The people could still see the smoke and fire of the Lord upon the mount. A few days earlier they had stood at the foot of the mountain and heard with their own ears the voice of God calling out from within the cloud. They heard God say, "*I am the Lord your God, who brought you out of the land of Egypt…You shall not make for yourself a carved image—any likeness of anything that is in heaven above, or that is in the earth beneath, or that is in the water under the earth; you shall not bow down to them nor serve them. For I, the Lord your God, am a jealous God*" (Exodus 20:2-5).

It had been forty days since that time and their leader, Moses, had been lost to them in the smoke. They were unwilling to go before the Lord themselves so they demanded Aaron make them a god that could lead them. A god they could approach. Aaron cast an idol in the image of a calf, sat it before the people, and said, "*This is your god, O Israel, that brought you out of the land of Egypt!*" (Exodus 32:4).

Aaron called the calf God and declared that he was the one who had brought the people out of Egypt. He hadn't made the people a new god, but an image of their God. One they could understand and approach. The people were afraid of God after their encounter with Him at the mountain. They witnessed the thunder and lightning and trembled in fear as they stood afar and said, "*You speak with us, and we will hear; but let not God speak with us, lest we die*" (Exodus 20:18-21).

They didn't want to stand before God again. They would rather Moses go on their behalf while they stayed away. One of the saddest scriptures in the whole of the Bible is found here. "*So the people stood afar off, but Moses drew near*" (Exodus 20:21). God's desire has always been for relationship with His people. This was why He brought them out of Egypt and to His mountain. Instead of drawing near, they ran in fear.

The people rejected God and instead crafted, concocted, and carved out a creation of their own hands and called it God. This god they understood, and this god they could control. Today people would rather serve their own idea of God as well. We can craft our own notions of who He is but the consequence of such thinking only creates our own golden calf we falsely label by His name. What happens when the fog is lifted from our eyes and we see our Creator shining forth for who He is? On that day we will realize God is far greater than we could ever imagine and He supersedes any idea we could create about Him. He is an awesome God!

The secret place is hidden within His awesomeness. Though we have access to boldly come before His throne, we must do so in reverent holy fear. He is still an all-consuming fire. He still dwells in unapproachable light. It is still a fearsome thing to behold Him.

The rebellion of the Israelites brought the nation to a perilous place. The Lord brought them to Himself, yet the people rejected Him. Now He commanded Moses to take the people away. He would still honor His promises to take them to the Promised Land, but would not go with them. The Lord said to Moses, "*Depart and go up from here, you and the people whom you have brought out of the land of Egypt, to the land of which I swore to Abraham, Isaac, and Jacob...and I will send My Angel before you...go up to a land flowing with milk and honey; for I will not go up in your midst, lest I consume you on the way, for you are a stiff-necked people*" (Exodus 33:1-3).

Moses knew this arrangement was not in the nation's best interest. If God would not go with them, he would not go. He stepped forward to make intercession on behalf of the nation and made his case before the Lord. *"If Your Presence does not go with us, do not bring us up from here. For how then will it be known that Your people and I have found grace in Your sight, except You go with us?"* (Exodus 33:15-16). The Lord looked with favor upon Moses and responded, "*I will also do this thing that you have spoken; for you have found grace in My sight, and I know you by name*" (Exodus 33:15-17).

Moses successfully interceded on behalf of his people. Having prevailed in prayer it might have seemed reasonable to conclude here, but Moses wasn't in a hurry to leave the king's presence. He was here because the people feared to come close. He would not make the same mistake. The Lord had given him favor; he was prepared to use it. He stepped forward and made an even bolder request: *"Please, show me Your glory"* (Exodus 33:18).

Moses had first met God here at this mountain. He saw the Lord from within the burning bush. He had returned to the mountain. This time instead of a bush ablaze the mountain was aflame. Now if he had to leave this place of transformation he longed to look beyond the flame and see the glory of God. He hungered for more and wanted to gaze upon God.

A. W. Tozer once said that the most important thing about a person is their view of God. Your view of God shapes everything about you. If you see God as a myth or fable, you'll live your life as though He does not exist. If you see God as a harsh deity with a lightning bolt in hand ready to smite the evil sinner, you'll serve Him in fear. If you see God as an all-loving God who would never punish sin, you'll likely embrace a false notion of grace that covers you in your sin, but never calls you to be free from sin. Truly the most important thing about you is your view of God.

We must see Him for who He is, not who we want Him to be. To know God and be known by God is the highest pursuit of man. To know Him, you must spend time with Him—that is the only way to ever know someone. It's a shame that so many people only know God in theory or through theology. They can tell you all about Him, but they don't know Him. Your view of God will be shaped by what you see and hear in the secret place.

The Lord's answer to Moses's request to see His glory was yes. He said, "*I will make all My goodness pass before you, and I will proclaim the name of the LORD before you...here is a place by Me, and you shall stand on the rock. So it shall be, while My glory passes by, that I will put you in the cleft of the rock, and will cover you with My hand while I pass by. Then I will take away My hand, and you shall see My back; but My face shall not be seen*" (Exodus 33:19-23).

The Lord said, "Beside me is a cleft in a rock." This was a secret place where God allowed Moses to abide. There the Lord covered Moses with His hand and passed by. Moses glimpsed the glory of God. Moses came down from the mountain and while the experience was still fresh on his mind he begins to write, "*He who dwells in the secret place of the Most High shall abide in the shadow of the Almighty.*"

That moment was short lived but the effects lasted a lifetime. Moses was marked by that encounter in the secret place. His face became so radiant that it emanated with the glory he had simply glimpsed upon. Moses left the mountain, but the mountain did not leave him.

My friend you have as much of God as you want. He has not limited you. Those who settle for little will ultimately lose what little they have. Those who long for more find there is so much more. The people wanted a distant knowledge of God while Moses wanted a closer fellowship. They could only tell you what they had seen from afar and that knowledge led them astray. Moses wrote of what he saw up close.

Don't grow content with your present relationship with the Lord. The secrets of Moses' secret place show us there is more. Contentment is a cancer to your soul that slowly eats away at your spiritual life, devouring the possibilities presented each and every day. The content will never contend for more. They always choose personal comfort over the surpassing glory.

Yes, pursuing God is strenuous but nothing else could ever be more rewarding.

Moses left a page from his journal for us to take to our own secret place. His words sparked a fire within my own life that has burned for over a decade. That same spark is ready to be set loose in you.

There is a door standing open to the secret place. Inside awaits the secrets of God's kingdom. Through Jesus there is a dimension of glory available to us that not even Moses could enter. Regardless of where you are with the Lord, I can assure you, there is more waiting for you.

Let those with ears to hear...let them hear!

> *Lord, I long to find You in the secret place. Help me to make You my dwelling place. May I be satisfied in You and find everything I need. Teach me Your ways that I might know You. Open my eyes that I might see You. My greatest desire is to gaze upon You and to hear Your voice as You speak. Lord, I am listening!*

NOTE

1. Leonard Ravenhill, *Why Revival Tarries* (Minneapolis, MN: Bethany Fellowship, 1959), 23.

About Daniel Norris

A true son of revival, Daniel Norris has been instrumental in bringing the message of repentance and reformation to the nations. His charismatic style and honest approach make him a favorite speaker among audiences of all ages. As an evangelist, his passion is to see the church experience the power and presence of God and to see communities experience the love of Christ.

After graduating from the Brownsville Revival School of Ministry, Daniel and his wife, Jenna, teamed up with evangelist Steve Hill to help plant Heartland World Ministries Church in the Dallas/Fort Worth Metroplex. For ten years they served as the directors of Redline Student Ministries, growing the youth ministry from nothing to over 350 students in just under three years. There Daniel launched the

Collision Youth Conference that has ministered to thousands around the US and has been seen by millions worldwide.

Not only has Daniel been honored to lead thousands to the cross through outreach events, he has also helped pioneer several Internet technologies that have reached multitudes around the world. These resources are helping lost sons and daughters come home every day to the loving arms of our Savior. In addition, Daniel assisted in the establishment of a two-year Bible school in the Dallas/Fort Worth Metroplex that placed ministers around the globe as pastors, evangelists, and missionaries.

Daniel is known to many as a pastor, evangelist, missionary, producer, and author, but he considers his greatest title to be Dad. He and Jenna live just north of Dallas, Texas, and have three beautiful children named Reijah, Caden, and Chase.

He welcomes your interaction and would love to connect at any of the following:

www.danielknorris.com

facebook.com/danielknorris

twitter.com/danielknorris